A Walking Guide to York's City Walls

Written for Friends of York Walls by **Simon Mattam**

First edition 2014 published by Eboru Publishing.

ISBN 978 0 9929002 0 5

Ordering Information: Quantity sales. Special discounts are available on quantity purchases by corporations, associations and others. For details, contact the publisher at the address below.

Orders by trade bookshops: copies of this book can be ordered direct from the publisher or through the normal wholesalers.

For any queries please contact enquiries@eboru.com

www.eboru.com

The publisher gratefully acknowledges the permission of copyright holders to reproduce copyright material:

p.59, 66, 92 © Alan Fleming; p.8, 22, 25, 53, 62, 68, 70, 71, 72, 75 © David Patrick; p.87 © Sunderland Museum and Winter Gardens.

All other photographs and illustrations are © Simon Mattam.

The publisher would like to thank Marie and Jim Gell for their enthusiasm and love for York, old and new.

See our Facebook page:
www.facebook.com/walkyorkwalls

AUTHOR ACKNOWLEDGEMENTS

(And access points for further information)

Friends of York Walls is a free membership organisation. Its first chairman, Keith Myers, asked me to write this book and many members have helped me. In particular Warwick Burton let me use what he had written for his professional York Walk guides and commented invaluably on my drafts. Alan Fleming gave useful advice, set up, with Richard Stroughair, the updates for this guide (see FoYW website: http://yorkwalls.org.uk) and provided the photographs on pages 59, 66 & 92 (he has made a collection of his and others' photographs of the Walls publicly available on www.flickr.com/groups/scenefromthewalls/pool/)

My most important written source is Royal Commission on Historical Monuments (England): "An inventory of the Historical Monuments in the City of York. 2: The Defences" (1972. HMSO, London). More readable, with a full bibliography and many old pictures of the Walls, is Barbara Wilson and Frances Mee: "The City Walls and Castles of York – The Pictorial Evidence" (2005. York Archaeological Trust, York).

I would like to thank:

John Oxley, City of York Council archaeologist, who patiently answered many questions.

David Patrick who has freely let me – and helped me – use his pictures of the Walls; the reproductions here do not do justice to the originals (his website www.davidpatrick-art.com does more justice).

Sunderland Museum and Winter Gardens for very efficiently providing and allowing use of the 'Hudson For Ever' image on p.87.

The Richard III Museum, who let me take and use the photograph on page 27.

The Gatehouse Cafe, who let me take and use the photographs on page 113.

Simon Mattam 2014

CONTENTS

Historical Map of the Trail

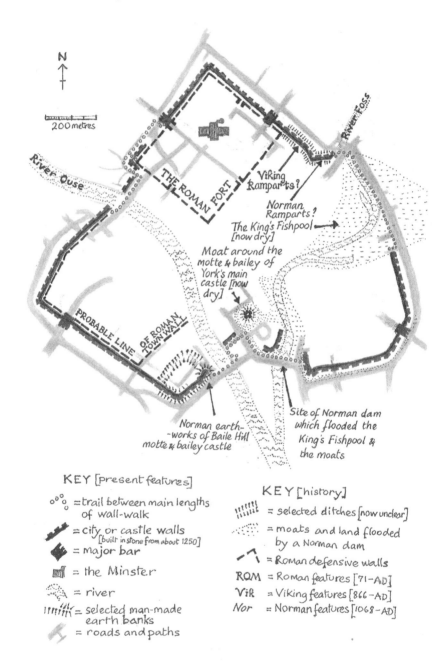

N
↑

200 metres

River Ouse

River Foss

THE ROMAN FORT

Viking
Ramparts?

Norman
Ramparts?

The King's Fishpool
[now dry]

Moat around the
motte & bailey of
York's main
castle [now
dry]

PROBABLE LINE OF ROMAN TOWN WALL

Norman earth-
-works of Baile Hill
motte & bailey castle

Site of Norman dam
which flooded the
King's Fishpool &
the moats

KEY [present features]

°°°°° = trail between main lengths
of wall-walk

= city or castle walls
[built in stone from about 1250]

= major bar

= the Minster

= river

= selected man-made
earth banks

= roads and paths

KEY [history]

= selected ditches [now unclear]

= moats and land flooded
by a Norman dam

= Roman defensive walls

RQM = Roman features [71–AD]

Vik = Viking features [866–AD]

Nor = Norman features [1068–AD]

INTRODUCTION

OVERVIEW

York still has most of the walls that surrounded the city 700 years ago. The tops of these were partly rebuilt about 150 years ago so the public could walk along most of them and feel safer by having a tall parapet on one side of them. Most think these are the best city walls in Britain – some say they give us the best city walk in Britain. In York – and in this guide – these are usually just called "the Walls".

This guide is to help you enjoy a circular walk that is on top of the Walls wherever possible. The route between these lengths of wall is marked on the ground with small brass pavement studs showing a tower with battlements.

Pavement studs mark the trail

Of course, this guide can also help you select particular sections of the Walls to walk on because there are about a dozen places where you can climb up to (or down from) the Walls. In this guide descriptions follow a clockwise direction around the Walls but they can be walked in either direction.

The information in this book mainly explains what you can see but there are a few historical stories for those who want to know what these walls have "seen", even if these events have left no obvious physical trace for you to see today.

1

The information here was checked in the winter of 2013/4; please tell us if you discover any mistakes or anything that has changed since then – for contact details and for the latest updates on information in this guide see the Friends of York Walls website (**http://yorkwalls.org.uk**) or this book's Facebook page **www.facebook.com/walkyorkwalls**

Walking the trail around the Walls is roughly like walking the edge of a kilometre square (but more interesting than this sounds!). Each side in this square has a grand medieval fortified gateway called a "bar". The trail is divided by these bars into four unequal corners.

Map of the Trail

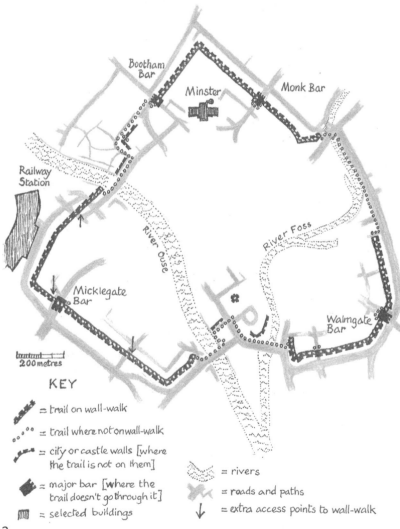

Bootham Bar

Minster

Monk Bar

Railway Station

River Ouse

River Foss

Micklegate Bar

Walmgate Bar

200 metres

KEY

= trail on wall-walk

= trail where not on wall-walk

= city or castle walls [where the trail is not on them]

= major bar [where the trail doesn't go through it]

= selected buildings

= rivers

= roads and paths

= extra access points to wall-walk

North Corner: The Minster

The corner that points north is the smallest and neatest corner, the only corner where the trail is always on the Walls. It is dominated by views of York's large and beautiful cathedral church, views often glimpsed through mature trees. It is the most walked corner; the wall-walk here has railings or a wall on both sides and several of the towers (low, open topped and open backed, like all interval and corner towers) have benches.

East Corner: Mix and Marsh

One part of this corner's Walls is like a continuation of the wall in the north but there is also a twisting part, a lowish part with no railings and, uniquely, a tower made of brick built in the Walls. There is no wall at all where the corner angle should be because there was once a big marshy lake here; at this point the trail runs beside a river. The buildings you pass by are a mix of church and state, domestic and commercial, Roman, medieval, Georgian, Victorian and modern.

South Corner: Castles and Crossings

This corner is the longest. Overall it is shaped like a corner with the angle 'punched in' where the Walls stop to cross two rivers and where there are the remains of two castles. Six roads cross the line of the trail in this corner (more than in the other three corners put together) and three of these crossings have the remains of medieval gateways.

West Corner: Railways and Ruins

This corner is in two stages: south of the River Ouse the wall-walk climbs to its highest near York's much admired Victorian railway station. Here it goes over arches built to provide access to this station – and over arches built to let trains get into York's previous railway station! North of the River Ouse the trail runs beside the Walls; Roman walls and other picturesque ruins are set in public gardens here.

The Bars

If you are selecting just parts of the Walls to walk then it helps to know more about the four main bars you will be choosing between, though they are all fine medieval buildings.

Bootham Bar

This is in the north-west, it has the best setting of any bar (when viewed from outside the city – the best view of any bar is usually from the front, from outside the city). It is the only bar where the free trail takes you through the room above the bar's archway and where that archway is still the main way through the Walls at that point.

Monk Bar

This is in the north-east, it is the tallest and strongest bar. It is the only one with its original medieval wall and windows surviving on the city side. It is the only one where you use the steep, low-ceilinged internal stairs to get to the wall-walk. If you pay you can go into its museum to see its portcullis (complete with the mechanism to wind it up and down) and medieval toilet.

Walmgate Bar

This is in the south-east and it is said to be the only city gate in England which still has its barbican. It is the only York bar where you can see clearly the (possible) scars of military attacks on it. If its café is open then you have access to its rooms and to the wall-walk around its barbican (as well as to fair-priced coffee and cakes! For details see "Refreshments, Seats & Toilets" on page 112).

Micklegate Bar

This is in the south-west and it is probably the most pictured bar. It is the bar where royal visitors are regularly greeted and there is a fine view into York from above its arch. If you pay you can enjoy its well-presented, informative museum.

The Lesser Gateways: Fishergate Bar, Victoria Bar and Fishergate Postern

These can also claim to be medieval gateways into York but they are much less impressive. At Fishergate Bar and Fishergate Postern you can see interesting medieval stonework. Friends of York Walls sometimes open the tall, roofed tower which guarded the postern (for details see http://yorkwalls.org.uk).

ACCESS TO THE WALL-WALK AND TRAIL

This guide is to help you enjoy a circular route that is on top of the Walls wherever possible. Sadly, no section on top of the Walls is suitable for use in a wheelchair (there are steps to go up, frequent steps along the walk and it's too narrow for safe passing). It is not ideal for pushchairs for the same reasons, although occasionally people try to use them. Dogs (other than guide dogs and assistance dogs) are banned.

The route between the walks on the Walls is marked on the ground with small brass pavement studs - see the photograph on page 1. This studded route is mainly on the flat and the steps that do exist are avoidable. This route can be made into a full circuit of the Walls – nearly always by going along the pavement on the Walls side of the roads which ring the Walls. The roads are often busy and some sections of the pavement are busy too but there is often a good view of the Walls. A short but very good part of the studded route goes through the beautiful Museum Gardens, which are usually freely open during the day (until 8pm in the summer).

The Walls are open (and free) to walk on from about 8.00am to dusk except when snow or ice is believed to make them dangerous. In normal conditions they are not usually scary for people with a medium fear of heights.

The trail on the Walls is closed for snow and ice

To find out more about their opening visit the City of York Council's website (then search for "City Walls"). For information on short notice closures, like those for ice, phone City of York Council's city centre department on 01904 552273 or their mobile 07983 956500 – they aim to be available 7.30 to 3.30 every day. Alternatively call into the VisitYork premises, on the corner 100 metres south of Bootham Bar.

You can walk either way round the Walls and can get up to them by the steps at the four main bars, at the 3 minor gateways, at the four other places where the wall-walk ends and, oddly, from a sort of large island in between some main roads 200 metres east of the railway station. To find these steps: start at the front of the railway station, and with your back to the station go to your left and cross the zebra crossings. Then continue along the pavement in front of the Victorian station hotel and its grounds until you come to a road junction controlled by traffic lights. Cross the road on your right first but then turn left at the traffic island to cross again so you get to the pavement with a statue and then go under the Walls and the steps are on your left.

BRIEF HISTORY OF THE WALLS

The Romans founded York around 71 AD. They built walls around their fort and then around the city that grew up on the other side of the River Ouse. Parts of the walls of the Roman fort can still be seen and up to half of the rest are in the ramparts under the present walls. 400 years later there were new invasions: Anglian York developed, then Viking York in the 9th century, then Norman York in the 11th century; over this time the Roman walls fell but earth ramparts grew.

About 900 years ago, the times we call "the Middle Ages" began – these were when the present Walls were built, mainly to protect York against attacks from the Scots. Around 500 years ago the Middle Ages ended and the introduction of cannon made the Walls less secure but they were strengthened in the 1640s for the English Civil War. The Walls were seriously attacked and damaged in this war of King against parliament but luckily a conditional surrender of the city stopped further damage and the parliamentarian victors arranged their speedy repair.

About 200 years ago there was another sort of battle being fought in York – over whether the Walls should be knocked down to open up the city to traffic and fresh air. During Victorian times a compromise developed: small sections of wall were demolished and new arches were built through the Walls but most of the Walls were repaired and opened as a footpath. Little has changed since then.

A more detailed history of the Walls is in the form of a time line at the end of this guide. Sixteen stories from the history of the Walls are separately labelled as stories at the end of the descriptions of a relevant section of the trail.

THE TRAIL

Introduction

In this part of the guide the trail is divided into 13 sections starting at Bootham Bar, the north-west gate. Each section starts with the "Basics" – these are for every reader, including those who want to walk the Walls speedily (taking, perhaps, little more than an hour to walk the whole trail). "Basics" are followed by "Details" – details about sections of the Walls in question. Next come the "Views" – describing things that can be seen from the trail but are beyond the Walls and ramparts. "Off-trail extras" are mainly less than 100 metres walk from the trail and many of these bring their rewards within 20 metres – but they are for you to select which to explore. Last come the brief "Stories" – these are true history as far as I can be sure, with the obvious exception of the last! They are certainly truer than the story you may have seen in the award-winning film "Braveheart" (2002) where Scots patriot William Wallace is shown leading an army that storms over York's Walls. The Walls were never stormed and Wallace's army did not even get to York.

MAP OF TRAIL PARTS 1-3

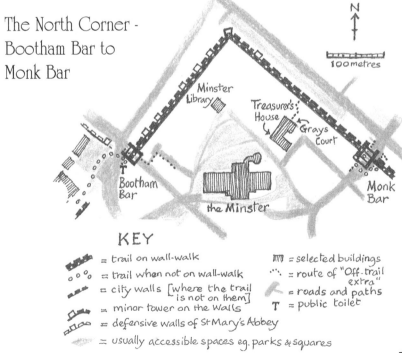

The North Corner - Bootham Bar to Monk Bar

N
100 metres

Minster Library
Treasurer's House
Grays Court
Bootham Bar
the Minster
Monk Bar

KEY

= trail on wall-walk
= trail when not on wall-walk
= city walls [where the trail is not on them]
= minor tower on the Walls
= defensive walls of St Mary's Abbey
= usually accessible spaces eg. parks & squares
= selected buildings
= route of "Off-trail extra"
= roads and paths
T = public toilet

THE TRAIL: 1. BOOTHAM BAR

Basics

This bar is best seen from the square outside it. This square is at the end of the trail so is also described in section 13. The square is separated from the Bar by a busy road; the traffic lights can help you cross safely but they will also test your patience. This view of the bar, and the red roofs and the Minster beyond, is very popular.

Looking from here you can see the oldest visible part of the bar – the round Norman arch (about 900 years old) and the medieval fort above it (about 700 years old) with its cross-shaped slits for arrows to be shot from. The remains of a Roman gateway here are under the ground. In the 19th century the bar was heavily repaired, the steps up to it were added and the three stone figures on the top were replaced. The trail goes up these steps, through the heavy, anti-pigeon gate and into the room above the arch. A portcullis is on your left and a 19th century wall is on your right – the original builders had larger windows here, as they didn't expect attacks from the York side of the bar!

Bootham Bar from Exhibition Square (David Patrick)

8

THE TRAIL: 1. BOOTHAM BAR

Details

The square it is best to see Bootham Bar from is called Exhibition Square; other views from it and off-trail extensions from it are described within section 13 of the trail. The best view of the bar is probably from immediately below the statue, to its right. The statue is of a Victorian painter from York called William Etty and a model of the bar is behind his knee because he campaigned to protect the Walls and bars.

The painted stone shields on the front of the bar are modern replacements for ones that had become weathered. They show a royal coat of arms and York's coat of arms (gold lions on a red cross of St. George). The three statues on top of the bar are by a Victorian mason who had his workshop beside the bar. They show a medieval lord mayor, knight and mason, and they replaced earlier statues.

There are information boards about the bar and the gateway of the Roman fort that is underground here.

The room at the top of the steps shows obvious signs of a floor above it (below the present ceiling level).

Carved and painted shields on Bootham Bar

Views

From the top of the steps going up to the bar: look down the steps, then up and a little to the right to see to see where the Walls start again. This is about 100 metres away on the other side of the road, which was built through the Walls by the corporation in the 1840s. To the right of this is the King's Manor, built around the house of the abbot of St Mary's Abbey (confiscated by King Henry VIII in 1539), then the statue of William Etty is in the middle of the square and, on the right of the square, the postern tower and defensive walls of St Mary's Abbey. Etty is shown looking at the bar because he was a leader in the fight to save the Walls from the corporation and for use as a public path. He is shown painting as he was a professional artist. He did paint the Walls but is better known for his nudes. Behind him is York Art Gallery.

From the 19th century slit windows: you can look into York along Petergate, one of York's picturesque, mostly car-free streets. This street follows the line of one of the two main roads running through the Roman Fort; it is not quite as straight a line as it was 19 centuries ago.

Petergate from the trail through Bootham Bar

Off-trail extras: 1. Toilets

The toilets are through their own doorways in the Walls a few metres either side of the steps going up to the bar. They are due to be redesigned and a 40 pence charge introduced during 2014.

Off-trail extras: 2. Precentor's Court

The court is a lovely, quiet street of Georgian housing 50 metres from the bar and if you go down it another 50 metres you get a splendid progressive view of the west front of the Minster (but you may then be tempted away from the trail along the Walls). To get to the court, walk under the main arch of the bar (watch out for traffic and look up to see the spikes of the portcullis and perhaps notice the coarse sandstone of the outer archway, put up 900 years ago and scraped by traffic ever since), go 20 metres down Petergate into York then go up a passage to your left just before the modern but Georgian-style "Hole in the Wall" pub. Then you can enjoy the sight of the real Georgian houses at the end of this passage. The west end of the Minster appears if you go down this quiet street. A precentor, after which this court is named, is the person in charge of music in a cathedral.

Georgian housing in Precentor's Court (off-trail extra)

Stories: 1. The battle of Myton

700 years ago Scotland was fighting its war of independence against England. At this time York sometimes seemed like the capital city of England: parliaments met here, the treasury was kept here and the King and Queen were often here. Edward II was King of England and he was particularly unsuccessful in war (his statue in the Minster shows him examining his finger nails, while his father stands beside him with his sword erect).

In 1319 events started to look a little like a game of chess: King Edward was besieging the Scots King on the Scottish border when a Scots force led by "Black Douglas" moved south to York in an attempt to capture the English Queen. They got to the gates of Bootham Bar, and burned the houses outside it, but they turned back when they discovered that the Queen had gone further south. The archbishop of York, the Lord Mayor and a force of priests and townspeople then chased after the Scots. The York "army" were unwise to leave the protection of the Walls and they were heavily defeated by the Scots at the battle of Myton-on-Swale. The Lord Mayor and 3,000 English were killed.

Immediately after this, York started to strengthen its city walls. The last sections of wooden wall were rebuilt in stone and barbicans were added at the front of the bars. Almost 200 years later the Scots were still seen as a problem in York, so the corporation ordered a "hammer" for the gate at every bar – any Scot wishing to enter the city was meant to knock with it to get special permission before coming through the bar.

Edward II seems to examine his nails

Stories: 2. Two Sheriffs

In 1503 Princess Margaret, daughter of King Henry VII of England, was leaving York for Scotland and her marriage to King James IV of Scotland. She was escorted through Bootham Bar and then down Bootham by the most important local officials. They were meant to be offering her their respect and protection but it seems they were more concerned with jockeying for position and competing with each other.

It is recorded that the sheriff of Yorkshire, appointed by the King to have authority in the county, acted as if he had left the city once he had left the city walls behind him. To be precise he raised his staff of office upright and higher than the staff of the sheriff of York (who was appointed by city leaders, thanks to a royal charter of 1396). This disgusted the sheriff of York because the city of York stretched further than the obvious, defensible boundaries of the city – and so his official authority stretched further than the obvious, defensible boundaries. Inside the city its sheriff had the legal power and he demanded that he should be allowed to show this by holding his staff higher. He complained to the Lord Mayor who told the sheriff of Yorkshire that the city continued to the Burton Stone about 400 metres away. So the sheriff of Yorkshire was compelled to lower his staff to the horizontal, along the side of his horse, until the boundary stone was reached. At this point the sheriff of Yorkshire raised his staff again and insisted that the sheriff of York's staff was lowered for the next part of Princess Margaret's journey.

Some people think that the Walls, like the sheriffs' staffs, came to be more about city pride than defence; this pride was linked to a sort of civic advertising. The Walls and bars made the statement "York is a wealthy and well organised city, where it is worth doing business".

THE TRAIL: 2. NORTH CORNER

Basics

You will be walking on a wall-walk built by the Victorians, beside battlements they rebuilt on walls that are basically medieval. These walls are on an earth rampart that was started by the Romans but then grew to cover what was left of the Roman wall.

This is the Minster corner: look to your right for many glimpses of the Minster as you walk along. The present Minster took 250 years to build so it has windows of all the three major Gothic styles, "early English", "decorated" and "perpendicular". First you see glimpses of the "decorated" style of the lovely "heart of Yorkshire" window at the west end and then the "perpendicular" style of its towers, built 100 years later. Just before you get to a corner tower on the Walls (known as Robin Hood Tower), you have the first good view of the Minster. The simple, spear-shaped, windows in the central, closest part of the Minster are the oldest ones in the present building – they are in the "early English" style of the 1220s. The large garden below you at this point belongs to the dean, who is in charge of the Minster and its grounds.

Robin Hood Tower is Victorian. The small slit windows you can see in its battlements could never be aimed out of with any success. This tower has benches and a good view of the next bit of wall and the ditch outside it. This view reminds us that there was once a deeper ditch all round the Walls.

The Minster and its library from the Walls

The top of the next tower was also built by Victorians – with two pretty, but very silly, little turrets. About 70 metres further on there are steps that lead down to a splendid house and garden. Around here the second good view of the Minster starts. The steps lead to Grays Court, a hotel which usually welcomes non-residents to their garden and parlour bar for drinks, teas and light lunches. In the 1880s, the owner of this garden and the dean reluctantly gave up what they saw as "their" bit of the Walls (and a bit of their privacy) to complete the trail you are now on.

At the end of this corner you see and enter Monk Bar, the next section of the trail.

Ditch, ramparts and Walls from Robin Hood Tower

THE TRAIL: 2. NORTH CORNER

Details

The first part of the Walls here didn't have a full stone wall-walk in medieval times – it probably had a narrow ledge that could be used to support a timber wall-walk in times of danger. The walls were also defended from interval towers which were higher than they are now after the Victorian restoration. These towers were usually open at the back – as their lower versions are now. The towers stick out from the walls so defenders on them could see the sides of those attacking the walls and deliver what is called "enfilading fire". The first five towers are relatively close together, perhaps because there was no permanent wall-walk here for defenders.

The Victorians built the wall-walk on arches and rebuilt the battlements and sometimes the top part of the Walls. We know that they took advice from experts in medieval military architecture so it is odd that they included features that would have brought problems to medieval defenders. Some slit windows are at the wrong height and some are narrow for the full width of the parapet – so that aiming through them would be almost impossible. Perhaps the rebuilders only wanted the Walls to look good from the outside – or in some places were just cutting corners and in others were trying to entertain.

Robin Hood Tower, at the angle of this corner, is a Victorian replacement for a ruined medieval tower which had had this name from about 1600 (unfortunately Robin Hood was a popular folk hero hundreds of years before this and we know of nothing that links him to

The ramparts and tower 28 in daffodil time

16

this tower). The tower has a carving of crossed keys set into its paving to remind us that it's close to the Minster (which is dedicated to St Peter who the Bible says was given the keys of heaven).

This tower is all Victorian but sometimes you can see where the medieval stonework ends and the Victorian rebuild (or build) begins. You can do this if you look at the outside of the next tower – look at it from Robin Hood Tower or, better, from an embrasure just before the tower. (An embrasure is one of the low bits of a parapet with battlements). The "pepperpot turrets" on this tower seem to have been put on as a bit of fun. This tower also has a bench and what some think is a mason's mark on its steps, but, like most of the interval towers, it has no name (just a Royal Commission for Historical Monuments number: tower 28).

The wall-walk here may be older than the Victorian one to Robin Hood Tower but you can see a few stones in the battlements that look newly sawn. These were laid during very recent repairs – one (forming the top ledge of an embrasure just before the steps down to Grays Court Garden) is unusually orange, showing how variable in colour magnesian limestone is.

Fun-sized Victorian turrets on Tower 28

A little after the steps down to Grays Court's garden there is a plaque set in the battlements (see "Stories: Who owns the Walls?" on page 20). A little further and there's an image of a Roman helmet set into the paving of the wall-walk. For the whole of the north corner of the trail you walk along the line of the walls of the Roman legionary fort of Eboracum; this is why you have walked a neat right-angle. You started at the site of Eboracum's north-west gate and this helmet marks the site of its north-east gate. It is thought that York's north-east gate was moved to Monk Bar 700 years ago because Minster priests did not like a major route going through their part of the city.

Views

In the first 50 metres: you get glimpses of the top of the great west window of the Minster. It is nicknamed the "heart of Yorkshire" because its graceful stone tracery has a traditional heart-shape in the centre of it. More generally the tracery seems inspired by the shapes of leaves similar to those of the ash tree which partly blocks your view for the first 20 metres. On the north side of the Minster (which you will soon see) there are slightly earlier windows where the "decorated Gothic" tracery is very geometric. The bell towers at the west end of the Minster and the central tower were added a hundred years later, so their windows are in the style called "perpendicular" (so called because of the repeated uprights in the stone tracery, that sometimes make it look like panelling).

Glimpses of the Minster from just after Bootham Bar

After the first 50 metres: as you walk, you can soon look down on a complex, varied bit of open ground where medieval archbishops once had their palace. The inner ramparts here are wooded and look best in May when there are bluebells here. The main thing that is left from the archbishop's palace is its chapel, which is now the Minster library. You'll see glimpses of it to the left of the Minster but closer to you; it backs onto the dean's beautiful big garden. It is linked to a modern building of a similar size, shape and stone which is closer to you. This is its recent extension.

The excellent view of the Minster from just before Robin Hood Tower (at the angle of the north corner) is described on page 14.

From Robin Hood Tower with your back to the Minster: to your right, running beside the best bit of town ditch that we still have, is Lord Mayor's Walk. This street was laid out as a paved, tree-lined promenade in Georgian times. The old-looking building on the far side of this road is not as old as it looks – it was built in Victorian times for a college that has developed into York's second university. You can see some of the modern buildings of York St John University to the left of its old buildings; if you are tall you can glimpse almost a kilometre away, between the old and the new, the flat roofed, red-brick Rowntree's sweet factory. Together with the railways, sweet-making provided the main new jobs in Victorian York. This factory is still an important employer in York (they still make Polos and Kit-Kat here) but the Swiss international company, Nestlé, now owns what was once a York family firm.

From near the Roman helmet in the paving: the view here is interestingly complex but the more attractive view is from about 15 metres back along the trail. Outside the Walls you can see where the route of the main Roman road from the north east survives as a slight dip in the level of the ramparts and then a narrow alley (humbly called Little Groves Lane). If you look inside the Walls the line of this road runs by the left side of the linked complex of old buildings on your right. These were once all part of the house of the Minster's treasurer. There is a small street on this line but only a hint of it can ever be seen from the Walls (through a group of trees that mask a gap in the housing closest to you); this small street is called Chapter House Street because it runs towards the yard between the consecrated parts of the Minster and its chapter house. (The chapter house is its medieval business centre, octagonal with a tall pointed roof). This street – or rather a cellar under it because the ground level here has risen several metres since Roman times – is York's most famous ghost site (an internet search for "Harry Martindale" will give you further details).

Most of the houses you have passed, between you and the Minster, have housed Minster officials since the Middle Ages (several still do). You can see some of old parts of these houses but many of the oldest parts are hidden inside them.

If you look along the wall-walk in front of you then you see Monk Bar with its wild men threatening to throw stones from the top of its extra storey.

The Treasurer's House and Grays Court

Off-trail extras: Café and Garden

Half-way between Robin Hood Tower and Monk Bar, private steps go down to the garden of Grays Court Hotel. This hotel is described in "Basics" and in "Refreshments, Seats & Toilets". Currently the gate to the steps is usually closed but it can be opened if customers make arrangements in advance (telephone 01904 612614). You go up the grand steps from the garden to get to the parlour. If the steps down to the garden are closed the only entrance to Grays Court is at the end of a street called Ogleforth (first right off your road if you go into the city at the next bar, Monk Bar).

Stories: Who Owns the Walls?

In Georgian times some people started to appreciate York's defences as romantic ruins, ruins that reminded them of dangers that were gone. One family bought Clifford's Tower, York's big castle keep (see page 57-67), grew trees and bushes in and around it and used it as a pretty picnic place at the bottom of their garden. Along the length of the

Walls by the Minster people started to feel that "their" bits of the Walls were an attractive part of their garden.

Meanwhile for the Lord Mayor and corporation of York the Walls were often an annoyance – they seemed unsafe and expensive to repair and they made it difficult for carts and carriages to get into York. Around 1800 the corporation had a small section in the south knocked down. However the archbishop of York successfully sued them in the law courts – he demanded damages because he could no longer collect tolls from people going through a gate in the Walls to a fair he had the right to hold. The corporation petitioned parliament to give them the clear right to demolish the Walls but they had no success and a campaign started to save the Walls and create a public path along them. The campaign had its successes and by the 1830s the corporation was knocking down some bits and repairing others.

By the 1880s the city's leaders had a new problem. They had repaired and restored almost all of the Walls but they couldn't complete the circuit because in this north corner people with interesting ruins at the bottom of their garden did not want their romantic garden feature transformed into a newly repaired wall – certainly not into a wall with a walk-way from which the public could stare down into their once-private gardens. One of the gardens belonged to the dean and another to Edwin Gray who was the son of a Lord Mayor and was a lawyer; he said he would sue the city leaders for trespass if they tried to touch "his" Walls. However, somehow by 1887 a deal was done and the Walls were restored to the city and restored to a good state of repair. A public footpath was established along them and a plaque placed on the Walls by Grays Court just hints at the conflict involved. The hint is so subtle that one website currently tells visitors that the "awkwardly worded" plaque is to tell us that Edwin Gray is to be remembered for helping to get the Walls restored. Edwin Gray was made Lord Mayor of York a few years after the restoration.

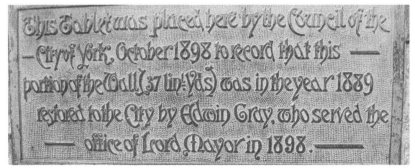

Gray's plaque

THE TRAIL: 3. MONK BAR

Basics

This bar is probably mostly 700 years old. If you approach it from the trail or the front notice the height of the bar and its arrow-slits as you approach. These, rather than the stone men hurling rocks from the top, help make it the strongest bar. The trail enters Monk Bar and turns right immediately to avoid a little museum with the bar's medieval toilet and a portcullis, complete with the machinery for winding it up and down. The trail goes down narrow, low-roofed, steep steps which contrast well with the 19th century steps to the pavement at Bootham Bar. The steps you go down seem designed for defence – and you'd have to cross to the other side of the bar, through a guarded room, to get to the steps that lead higher in the bar.

Turn left at street level and a brass trail stud in the pavement on your left suggests you should enter the bar's arch. Do this, though watch out for bikes from behind you, and on your right there is a blocked doorway in the wall, left from the times when traders would be stopped as they went through these bars and made to pay "murage". Murage was a tax on goods being brought into York for sale, a tax which went to pay for the Walls – and for the murage-collector who came through this door.

Walk through the arch and look up to see the spikes of the portcullis, waiting to slide down between its grooves and seal off the arch. Go a metre further and you can see above you the dark "murder holes" through which things could be dropped on anyone attacking the portcullis. If you are in a hurry its best now to retrace your steps to the city side of the arch and then to cross the road at the traffic lights – be careful: traffic may come from left or right. The trail continues on the next section of the wall via the steps in front of you.

Approaching Monk Bar (David Patrick)

THE TRAIL: 3. MONK BAR

Details

The top storey of this tall bar was probably added at the time of King Richard III during what are now called "the Wars of the Roses". He was probably York's favourite (and Shakespeare's least favourite) king and much of the museum in this bar is about him. For more about the museum, see below.

The "Basics" section mentions the space under the bar's main arch (the arches through the wall on either side of this are 19th Century). This medieval space is stone vaulted so it could resist attacks by fire. Several masons' marks have been recorded here, the easiest to find, shown below, is at eye-level, on the second stone to the right of the blocked up doorway. (More about such marks is at the end of the "Stone and Stonework" section in the Appendix.) In medieval times the ground under the portcullis would not have been paved as the points on the portcullis were to fix it firmly in the earth, not to pierce attackers caught underneath as it came down! A portcullis fixed in this way has none of the weak points of an ordinary door – no hinges or lock to give way. It is thought that every gate through the Walls once had a portcullis, but now Monk Bar's is the most complete.

Off-trail extras: 1. Monk Bar Museum

The small museum inside the bar is now run by the York Archaeological Trust. For a small entrance fee it tells you a lot about one of England's most controversial kings and it also lets you explore inside the bar.

A mason's mark at Monk Bar

You can see the bar's "garde-robe" (medieval toilet), the portcullis and its raising machinery, and you can see how it was designed to resist attack with narrow stairs on alternate sides of the bar and stone ceilings. You can also see the little turret room that was probably used as a prison, called "Little Ease" because even lying down would be difficult there. It is free to enter the first room, containing a small shop and the portcullis. For more details see the Richard III Museum's website: www.richardiiimuseum.co.uk

Off-trail extras: 2. Front of the bar

Walk about 15 metres past the portcullis and look back at the front of the bar (if the pavement is busy there's a small alleyway). High above the archway you can see the balcony for the defence of the portcullis below it. There are arrow-slits but in the centre towards the top you can see two small square holes with a small cross-shaped slit above each one. These are for cannon – the slits were used to aim them.

Monk Bar from the front (off-trail extra)

Near the corners, at the level of the lowest arrow-slits, are what look like small, metal studded, wooden doors, one at each side of the bar. They really are doors and only make sense when you realise that the bar had a barbican stretching out from it. These doors allowed the wall-walks of the barbican to be manned by defenders coming from the room above the bar arch. The barbican reached roughly to where you are standing. It had a gate that attackers would have to get through before finding themselves in what was called "the killing ground" – they would be faced, in the barbican, by a portcullis and surrounded by walls manned by defenders looking down on them. In the early 19th century all the bars except Walmgate had their barbicans demolished – mainly because they got in the way of traffic.

The painted stone shields on the front of the bar are a royal coat of arms from the mid-Middle Ages and York's coat of arms – see the photograph on page 9.

Off-trail extras: 3. Back of the bar

If you go 10 or so metres into York from the bar the street is often busy but you can look up at the only medieval back wall to a bar that York still has. You can see that it has proper windows rather than arrow-slits, as the bar was designed to be defended against attacks from outside York and doubled as a home in the Middle Ages. Rents from the use of the bars as homes were one way money was raised to pay for the repair of the Walls. The balcony just above the arch is thought to have been used for public proclamations.

Monk Bar from inside the walled city (David Patrick)

Off-trail extras: 4. Pub Garden

As you look at the bar from the outside, the Keystones pub is on the corner on your left. This is an ordinary pub (part of the Scream chain) but its open air seating is extraordinarily well situated. To the right of the pub there is level access from the pavement to this eating and drinking area. From this area there is fairly level access to the pub's bar and its toilets (including one for the disabled). The area is well sheltered from the road and the weather; it is beside the outer ramparts, with excellent views of the Walls. An added interest here is a Georgian ice house built into the ramparts – for more details see page 31.

Pub garden, ice house and Walls near Monk Bar (off-trail extra)

Stories: Working Portcullis?

Monk Bar is often described as having a "working portcullis" – the English often like to be thought of as modest and masters of understatement, but this claim about the portcullis seems an exaggeration. Firstly, as the work of a portcullis is to seal off a gateway against attack, to say we have a working portcullis seems a worrying reflection on law and order in modern Britain. To be fair, most people probably take the claim just to mean that the portcullis goes up and down. However the portcullis certainly doesn't go up and down often at the moment. One information board at Monk Bar says that it went up and down weekly till 1970 but this seems to be a mistake. Most people say that regular lowering stopped before the Second World War.

It is true that the portcullis still seems to have much of the equipment that was once used to raise and lower it – in particular it has a long windlass or winch that can be turned by pulling on stakes inserted into it – but it is usually said that the last time anyone actually tried to use this equipment to lower the portcullis was in 1953, to celebrate the crowning of the Queen. Closing a medieval gate might be thought a slightly odd form of celebration but in any case it was not entirely successful. It is said that after the coronation local papers noted that it took 10 minutes to get it down but two weeks to get it up again. The story is that while the gate was being raised a chain pulling it up broke; some say that the side pulled by that chain fell, which jammed the whole heavy gate firmly into its stone slots, whilst others say the whole portcullis fell and buried its spikes deep into the tarmac of the road. In any case, simply fitting a new chain and pulling on it was not enough to release the jammed gate. Until very recently the problems encountered then seem to have deterred people from suggesting that this portcullis should be "worked" again, but in the spring of 2013 the suggestion arose once more – this time to mark the 60 years passed since the coronation. The then owner of the museum was not keen to try - but perhaps now we can hope for archaeological experiments.

The 'working' portcullis in Monk Bar, in 2013

MAP OF TRAIL PARTS 4-7

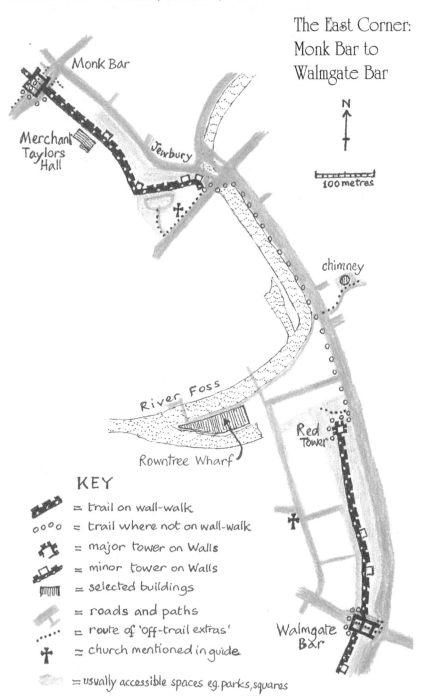

The East Corner:
Monk Bar to
Walmgate Bar

Monk Bar

Merchant
Taylors
Hall

Jewbury

N

100 metres

chimney

River Foss

Red
Tower

Rowntree Wharf

KEY

= trail on wall-walk

o o o o = trail where not on wall-walk

= major tower on Walls

= minor tower on Walls

= selected buildings

= roads and paths

..... = route of 'off-trail extras'

✝ = church mentioned in guide

= usually accessible spaces eg. parks, squares

Walmgate
Bar

28

THE TRAIL: 4. EAST CORNER PART 1

Basics

Part one of this corner starts with the roofless steps going up to the Walls at Monk Bar and ends where this section of Walls ends.

As soon as you get to the wall-walk you will see musket loops; these are probably from the English Civil War, to be aimed through by a kneeling man. The wall-walk you are on is probably from the late Middle Ages, though Victorians repaired it along with the battlements.

Very soon, on your left, you can see the brick dome of a Georgian ice house cut into the outer ramparts below you. At this point you also have a good view of a large medieval building partly cut into the inner ramparts ahead of you: this is the Merchant Taylors' Hall. The building looks duller as you get closer as it was mostly encased in brick by Georgian times. Between you and this guild hall archaeologists have cut into the inner ramparts and have left exposed a corner of the Roman legionary fort.

Roman, Medieval and modern buildings south of Monk Bar

Just past the guild hall, on the wall walk but partly behind railings, there is what's left of two toilets. These may well be medieval; opinions differ on who would have used them but they have been described as extremely public toilets. From this point the line of the Walls is less straight as it has left the ramparts the Romans started and is probably on Viking and then Norman ramparts. The next tower has been rebuilt by Victorians – with chimney-like little turrets. Outside the Walls near here you begin to see a three storey car park, which has been built on the site of York's medieval Jewish cemetery. The area is still called Jewbury but it was long uncared for as all Jews were expelled from England 700 years ago (only returning gradually after more than 300 years).

At the next tower (called "New Tower" since 1380) the Walls turn outwards to protect the medieval church of St. Cuthbert's. There is a small, quiet public garden immediately below you on the right and this is described in "Refreshments, Seats & Toilets" in the Appendix, and as an Off-trail extra on page 36. Just past the tower there are good views looking back to your left: a hint of a grassy ditch, the ramparts, the Walls and a little of the Minster.

Looking back when the Walls have swung east

THE TRAIL: 4. EAST CORNER PART 1

Details

Some say the musket loops were higher before the Victorian restoration and were for a musketeer standing with the gun against his shoulder. At least one of the loops, just after the steps up, seems to have been created by filling an embrasure in the battlements.

The place for the best view of the ice house is shown by an ice symbol set in the paving of the wall-walk. The house is a bit like an igloo in reverse. It is built with brick but is mainly underground and was made around 1800. It would be filled with ice in winter so that this could be used throughout the rest of the year for iced foods and drinks.

On the opposite side of the Walls at this point you can see you are immediately above the excavated remains of a Roman interval tower in the walls that surrounded the legionary fort 1800 years ago. The first excavation here was in late Victorian times and the last was in the 1930s. The hole the archaeologists have left gets deeper further along the Walls so there you can see a tall wall by the corner of the fort. You can see these towers do not stick out from the Roman walls so defenders in the towers could not have attacked hostile Britons from the side as they approached the walls: perhaps the Romans did not fear this sort of attack. There is an information board on the wall-walk's railings about the Roman walls.

The medieval guilds of York were part trade association, part charity and part religious fellowship; usually you had to join one if you wanted to do business in the city. Tailoring was one of the biggest trades in

Musket loop made from embrasure

medieval York: there were 128 master-tailors in 1386 when records started. These were the full members of the guild, allowed to employ journeymen (paid by the day) and apprentices who would usually live in a master's home. This is one of several medieval guild halls in York.

Views

From just past the guild hall: The wall-walk soon narrows so it may be best to look around you before you get to the best view of Jewbury – shown by a star of David set in the paving of the wall-walk. Most of the site of the cemetery is now covered by the Sainsbury's car park but you can see the modest, metre-high, red granite plaque commemorating the dead, set into the nearest part of the car park's red-brick wall; its story is told below. To the left of this is Georgian housing. Turn further to the left and you are looking back at the Minster. The modern housing between you and the Minster here is very popular, and is thought of as successfully bringing people back into the city to live. This was a major planning aim in the 1960s.

Looking forward you'll see the ramparts and Walls turn east and get lower – but the best view of these is about 25 metres further on where you can also see New Tower (round with long arrow-slits) and where the Walls and ramparts end with two older, more angular towers, the first with shorter "musket loops".

Stories: Respect in Jewbury

It is unusual for an old place name in York to be so clear and helpful but, partly by accident, the place where medieval Jews buried their dead in York has long been called Jewbury.

There was a thriving Jewish community in 13th century York. Its members must have felt vulnerable as their religion made them the only religious minority in the country and meant they were excluded from membership of the guilds which controlled most trade in the city. They must have known of the terrible end of the 12th century York Jews (see "The Saddest Story" on page 65).

The Jewish religion taught then – and still teaches now – that the dead and their bodies should be treated with the greatest respect. In this teaching, the passing of time does not alter the need for respect, so archaeologists have come to recognise Jewish cemeteries by the lack of graves cutting across and through much earlier graves; Jewish grave diggers seem to have been exceptional in the care they gave not to disturb human remains. (Incidentally Shakespeare seemed to want the same care for his grave when he wrote: "Good friend, for Jesus sake forbear to dig the dust enclosed here, blessed be the man that spares these stones and cursed be he that moves my bones"). But all Jews were expelled from England in 1290 so they could no longer take care of their cemeteries.

Almost 700 years later in York there were just a few documents that suggested that there was once a cemetery where holes were to be dug as part of new building in "Jewbury". Archaeologists were called in to investigate the site before builders started work; this respect for the archaeological evidence that might otherwise be destroyed by building is legally required everywhere in old York because it is a designated "Area of Archaeological Importance".

The archaeologists discovered about 500 medieval graves and the skeletons in them – and wanted to dig further and do tests on the bones and teeth to discover more about the diet and health of the times. But, in spite of the lack of gravestones and lack of traditionally nail-less Jewish coffins, the care that had been taken in the lay-out of the graves helped make the archaeologists and modern religious Jewish authorities in England believe that this was a Jewish cemetery. This being so, the archaeologists felt they should do as the Chief Rabbi wished. This ended their research as he said: "Whatever the scientific and historical loss... the dignity shown to humans even centuries after their death can contribute more than any scientific enquiry... to the respect in which human beings hold each other". The skeletons were removed to a Jewish mortuary and then returned to Jewbury for a burial supervised by the chief rabbi in 1984, 700 years or more after they were first buried.

Respect in stone: the wall-walk's sign points to Jewbury where the tablet in the brick wall marks a medieval graveyard (off-trail)

THE TRAIL: 5. EAST CORNER PART 2

Basics

Part 2 of this corner was once part of a large, marshy lake that neither the Walls nor attackers could easily cross. The trail in this part starts where you come off the Walls at a complex of road junctions and bridges and ends where the Walls begin again at Red Tower. This part of the trail heads more directly south than part 1 and, with part 3, cuts off the angle of the east corner by going in a single slight curve to the next bar.

You have three flows of traffic to cross using traffic lights: turn right as you get off the walls and cross left to a small traffic island, then turn right to cross two flows of traffic to the pavement on a bridge over the River Foss. Turn left and stay on the pavement, walking beside the river. The river you walk beside here was made into a great lake – called the King's Fishpool – by William the Conqueror around 1068 when he ordered it to be dammed to create a moat around his castle half a kilometre downstream. More than 700 years later the river was canalised and then Victorians raised the level of the silted up lake.

After a while the river curves to the right but you should walk straight on along the road. If you look down the river immediately after it has curved off to the right you'll see a towered, red brick Victorian warehouse come into view. Barges travelled on the Foss and unloaded here (most recently for Rowntree's sweet factory so it is called Rowntree Wharf). Now the warehouse has been converted into homes and offices – and it is mainly water birds that go up and down the river.

Soon you cross a side street called Navigation Road; soon after this you will see the Walls and you can get back on to them by going anti-clockwise round the Red Tower.

Greylag goose and ducks on what's left of the King's Fishpool

THE TRAIL: 5. EAST CORNER PART 2

Details

At the very start of this section of the trail there is an information board that shows how far the lake once spread from this point (the public toilets shown on this board have also disappeared now!). When the modern bridges were being built a cobbled Roman ford was found here – about five metres below the present bed of the river.

Before crossing the road you may wish to visit a hidden garden just off the trail – see "Off-trail extras: 1" on page 36.

Once you have crossed the Foss the trail along the pavement seems to have lost some of its way-marking brass studs when it lost its Victorian "York stone" paving slabs. Some find this the least interesting section of the whole trail but others call the Foss "the largest industrial archaeology monument in York"and remember that canals like this were the superhighways of Georgian times, vital for Britain's industrialisation.

Views

From just over the bridge: you can look back at the bridge itself and beyond this at the Walls you have left together with the Minster. The bridge, with its round tower-like extras, quietly echoes the Walls but

A lights-laden junction and the Walls echoed in Layerthorpe Bridge

the road junction itself has been criticised for its muddle of multiple mixed poles and lamp-posts. A little to the left of the Walls is the medieval church of St Cuthbert's but the buildings around you are late Victorian or later, built on what had been a marshy lake. The tall brick chimney, across the road in the opposite direction from the Minster, was for a Victorian waste-incinerator. If you look down the River Foss you can see an arched metal footbridge (usually closed) which leads to a small nature reserve by a quiet backwater. This reserve was used to reintroduce swans to the river in the 1990s. As well as swans you can probably now see moorhens, coots, ducks and geese. The geese which are grey and fawn, with no black, are "greylag geese"; in medieval times they came to England for the winters but then lagged behind when other geese left. Consequently farm geese were bred from them and they were hunted for food. The King's Fishpool didn't only provide bream and pike to eat, it also provided waterfowl like these.

From just after the arched metal footbridge on your right: you can look over the river and through the weeping willows to the nature reserve with its backwater and get a small impression of what this whole area was once like in summer, when the waters of the lake sank and many low islands appeared. The shallow lake stretched for about a hundred metres in front of you and more than 200 metres behind. The road that runs along the river here is called Foss Islands Road. It is part of what York calls its inner ring road, and is almost the only part that looks anything like the 4-lane road-around-the-Walls that some people were planning for York about 50 years ago; the plan was strongly opposed by local groups and it was defeated, partly because it was thought that such a road would be a poor setting for the Walls.

Off-trail extras: 1. Hidden garden

A small quiet, public garden just below and inside the Walls was mentioned on page 30 in the "Basics" section for the first part of this corner. It is an attractive space and has many benches. The two entrances are easy to miss and are about 80 metres from the Walls trail. As soon as you come off the Walls turn right and follow the pavement around instead of crossing the roads and bridge on your left. You will pass the medieval church of St Cuthbert's then find the entrances on your right, just before the Quilt Museum (which is housed in a medieval guild hall called St Anthony's Hall; the garden is called St Anthony's Garden).

As you reach the entrances you may be tempted by the look of the Black Swan, an old and popular half-timbered pub a little ahead of you

St Anthony's Garden (off-trail extra)

on the other side of the road – this is very understandable but at least have a look at the hidden garden first, it is lovely.

Off-trail extras: 2. Café

The café of Morrison's supermarket, with a toilet next to the café, is conveniently close to the trail. It could not be better signposted because it is at the bottom of the huge (by York's standards!) Victorian chimney you see to your left as you walk along the river. Leave the trail by a crossing to your left when you are just past the closest point to the chimney, then go up a short red-brick path till you get to the red-brick chimney. You'll see an entrance to the supermarket just in front of you. Inside there is everything you'd expect of this expanding, Yorkshire-based supermarket chain – even a small display about "the Destructor", the Victorian incinerator the chimney was built for (the Story below has more details). Morrison's originally wanted to write "Morrison's" down the chimney but was told this was not how York dealt with its historical heritage!

Off-trail extras: 3. Picnic benches

When you first see the Red Tower you will see a small garden between you and it – this is part of Rosemary Place. It has benches, picnic tables and a few things for young children to play on – and even some bushes of rosemary. You are surrounded here by some of the most conveniently placed council housing in York. It is allocated especially to people with mobility problems.

Rosemary Place and the Red Tower (off-trail extra)

Stories: York's rubbish

When William the Conqueror caused the great lake to form here it was called the King's Fishpool. Laws strictly limited who could fish the lake or even have a boat on it – and there were laws to try to prevent its being polluted by rubbish being dumped in it. Records say that in 1407 there was a 100 shilling fine for "throwing filth into the Foss to the prejudice of the royal fishery". This was at a time when half a shilling was the fine for fouling the River Ouse!

Medieval York was notorious for its problems with rubbish. In 1330 Edward III sent a clean-up order to York's mayor beginning: "The King, detesting the abominable smell abounding in the said city more than any other in the realm from the dung and manure and other filth and dirt wherewith the streets and lanes are filled and obstructed...". At one time the people who lived in the poor bit of the city beside the lake complained that they could not hear the priest in their parish church because of the noise of dogs fighting over the butchers' waste dumped outside.

In the early 19th century what was left of the lake was seen as a health hazard. It smelt and this was thought to be linked to sickness like the cholera epidemic of 1832. So instead of trying to keep the area clear of rubbish, the corporation decided to concentrate rubbish here to help build up the ground level – people were paid a bounty by the corporation if they dumped a cartload of rubbish in what was once the King's Fishpool.

When the ground level was thought high enough York people still brought rubbish here. In 1899 the big chimney was built for an incinerator which burnt the city's rubbish. It was called "the Destructor" but it did more than destroy because it was part of an early attempt at energy efficiency. The chimney was shared with an electricity generator and when rubbish was burned the heat was used to generate steam which worked a stone crusher, a mortar mixer and, if there was any energy left, the generator. Waste is still managed near here: 200 metres east of the chimney, where the edge of the lake once was, is York's central waste and recycling centre.

The Destructor's chimney and the River Foss

THE TRAIL: 6. EAST CORNER PART 3

Basics

At the Red Tower the Walls start again and the trail leaves the side of the road and goes right to join the wall-walk behind the tower. The tower was built of brick at the end of the Middle Ages when money was short in York and the corporation wanted to save money by using cheaper materials.

Victorians heavily repaired the ruined tower and built up the land around here (by about two metres) so the tower seems much lower than it did when it guarded the large marshy lake that reached up to it. Victorians also repaired the wall-walk and parapet of the Walls here but they noted that at least some of the cross shaped slit windows in the parapet were there before they started repairs. The wall-walk has few railings in this section.

On the city side of this part of the trail there is mainly council housing from the mid 20th century because in Victorian times this was an area of very poor housing. However, just after the first interval tower, at the end of the second little road you will pass on your right, there is a medieval, towered church; this is St Margaret's. This reminds us that the Walls were still protecting the old city here.

This section ends with Walmgate Bar, and fairly good views of the bar as you approach it; the next section of the trail begins as soon you get to the pavement.

Low ramparts and the Walls just north of Walmgate Bar

THE TRAIL: 6. EAST CORNER PART 3

Details

The Red Tower, built around 1500, is the only one in the whole trail to be built of brick rather than large blocks of magnesian limestone cut from quarries about 10 miles away. Much of modern York is built on clay so locally-made bricks were a much cheaper building material. (The Story for this part of the Walls goes into more detail). The part of the trail that goes around the tower goes under a "garde-robe" (toilet) that sticks out a little from the wall, but there is no longer the hole that would have allowed human waste to drop straight into the lake.

The Walls here protected the newest area of the walled city: the part that grew up about 800 years ago as the suburb of Walmgate, east of the River Foss on land that was just above the level of the King's Fishpool. The ramparts here have only had stone walls on them since the mid-14th century. The parapet defending the wall-walk is pierced by a mix of musket loops, cross-shaped arrow-slits and simple embrasures. Four hundred years after it was built the wall-walk here seems to have been one of the sections used as a recreational footpath, long before the Victorians did their restorations and established the present paved wall-walks on the Walls.

This is a good part of the walls for spotting the small brass markers embedded every 25 metres along the middle of the wall-walk. The easiest to spot are domed and a centimetre across (every 100 metres) whilst the others are smaller and flatter, circular or hexagonal – these are simply to help those involved in maintenance to map problems that need attention. Spotting them is one of the less rewarding ways to use your time on the Walls but it can be addictive!

The wall-walk widens into a rectangular interval tower less than 100 metres before Walmgate Bar, where a modern block of flats comes very close to the wall. The battlements of this tower have two cross-shaped arrow-slits in their merlons. (Merlons are the taller bits of a parapet with battlements.) Two other features here are easier to see from the photographs on the next page than from the walkway. Firstly the arrow-slits are crowned on the outside by a small stone gable. Most of the cross-shaped arrow-slits along this part of the corner have these unusual extras, which were noted before the Victorians did their restorations, but there seem to be more of them now than there were before the restorations. Secondly, below the paving of the tower, there are two sets of steps going down to the rampart – presumably these steps were once part of the early recreational wall-walk here.

A hooded arrow-slit, just north of Walmgate Bar

Arrow-slits and embrasures above steps for earlier walkers of the Walls

Views

The best views from around the Red Tower are of the tower and the Walls beyond it but as you walk along the wall-walk you can pause and look back at features that have already been mentioned: Rowntree Wharf (the red-brick Victorian warehouse with its battlemented tower), the Victorian incinerator chimney ("the Destructor") – and the Minster between them.

As mentioned in "Basics", at the end of the second little road to your right you can see a medieval, low towered church, it has large windows of decorated Gothic style; this is St. Margaret's. It was heavily restored by Victorians and then it became one of the many York churches converted to another use; it is now the National Centre for Early Music and this conversion won an architectural award.

Medieval St Margaret's amid the council housing that replaced Victorian slums

Stories: Murder at the Red Tower

Towards the end of the Middle Ages, in the mid-15th century, York became less prosperous. Ships were getting bigger and docking at Hull rather than coming up-river to York. Newer towns like Leeds, where the guilds were less powerful in controlling competition, were taking business away from York and from time to time there was open fighting over who should be King, fighting that was later called "the Wars of the Roses". For a while it seemed that York had a friend in the local man crowned as Richard III – he forgave York taxes and had plans to rebuild the castle but then he was killed and his enemy became King.

The new King Henry VII was given an expensive royal reception in York in 1486 but he was locally unpopular: in 1487 a rebellion against him made an unsuccessful attack on Bootham Bar and two years later attacks on Fishergate Bar and Walmgate Bar damaged them badly. In the 1490s the corporation decided it needed a tower built where the Walls ended south of the great marshy lake – but they decided they couldn't afford to have it built from stone by members of the masons' guild (a society of masons who controlled all work with stone in York). The corporation asked members of the tilers' guild to build the tower of bricks made locally.

Tilers started the work but they soon complained to the corporation that their tools were being broken or stolen. Officials of the masons' guild were sent for by the corporation and the language they used in their defence got them locked up in prison for the night. Then a tiler was murdered. An official of the masons' guild, the master mason at the Minster who was responsible for the great screen made of statues of the kings of England shown on page 12, was charged with murder. It is said that at first he couldn't be arrested by the city authorities because he stayed in area controlled by the archbishop (the Minster still has its own police). He seemed totally unashamed throughout this conflict, as it is said that while he was in prison he employed a man to shout news of his imprisonment through the streets of York so that all who had business with him should know where to find him. He was not convicted of the murder. The tilers finished the Red Tower but nearly all future work on the Walls seems to have been done in stone, by masons.

The Red Tower

THE TRAIL: 7. WALMGATE BAR

Basics

This is the only bar which still has its medieval barbican and which seems to show the scars of military attacks; you can see both from the pavement at the bottom of the steps leading off the Walls, north of the bar. The main bar building is above and in front of you and the blank wall of the barbican runs out to its left. If you look carefully at the bottom two courses of stone you'll see a crack and dip in them about a third of the way along the barbican's wall; this is thought to be the result of a mine dug under the bar in an attack in 1644 during the English Civil War – more details are in the Story for this section.

The trail continues by crossing the road at the traffic lights to your right. After crossing the road the steps up to the next section of the Walls are ahead of you but before reaching them you can look left, down through the bar's archway, to the roofless passage of its barbican. This passage was the defence provided by the barbican; if attackers broke through the gate that would have closed the far end of the barbican, they would come into this passage (or "killing ground") surrounded on all sides by manned walls above them as they continued towards the bar's portcullis and main gate. If you look carefully you can see that there are old wooden gates close on either side of you.

At the steps up to the next section of the Walls turn back to the bar to see the extension to its living space that was added at the time of Queen Elizabeth I – there is a café you can visit there. The same steps go to the café and to the next corner of the trail (with an excellent view back to the bar).

Walmgate Bar and its barbican from the north (off-trail extra)

THE TRAIL: 7. WALMGATE BAR

Details

Most of the details of this bar are given in two very short "Off-trail extras" but it is worth mentioning a possible link between all the modern buildings next to this bar and the survival of the barbican. In mid-Victorian times the councillor elected to represent this area (one of the Rowntree family) claimed that the council had failed to remove the barbican and improve the roads in this area because the people living in it were so poor that they were thought not to matter. He wanted the barbican and the Walls in this area to be knocked down to bring more space and cleaner air – but the Lord Mayor said he wouldn't want to be the man who removed the Walls' last barbican. Poor housing conditions around here were finally dealt with in the next century by the council buying, demolishing and building homes – this was called "slum-clearance".

Off-trail extras: 1. Barbican

From the back of the bar, go under the Elizabethan upstairs extension, past the great oak doors (probably 15th century), noticing the little wicket-gate within the main door on your left, go under the portcullis spikes – noticing the groove for the portcullis to slide down – and enter the "killing ground" mentioned in "Basics".

Go through this, turn left and look immediately at the outside face of this, the front wall of the barbican. At waist height, almost exactly in the middle of the wall, you should be able to see what looks like the result

Cannon ball scar at Walmgate Bar? (off-trail extra)

of a cannon ball from the east hitting the stone work: a hollow with radiating cracks. Some authorities say that this is the result of the 1644 bombardment.

The same stone has much smaller hollows that look as if they could be caused by musket balls but there are many more of these to be seen if you carry on round the corner a couple of metres and look up at the right hand corner-turret of the main bar, looking especially at the stones 7 to 12 courses directly below the little window. Again opinion seems divided, with some people thinking that all of the hollows are caused by natural weathering.

Musket ball scars at Walmgate Bar? (off-trail extra)

A few metres further and you are next to the dip (in the lowest courses of stone-work) that is mentioned in "Basics".

Your best way back to the trail is now to retrace your steps. The carving above the gateway where you re-enter the barbican could once be read as recording, below the city's coat of arms, that the barbican was restored in 1648. The carving above the archway of the bar commemorates a later restoration and is below a shield with a medieval royal coat of arms.

Off-trail extras: 2. Café

Above the arch the rooms of Walmgate Bar are occupied by a small, church-run café. Although it can sometimes be busy, it is a special visual treat, usually open 10.00 – 6.00 but not open on Sundays (phone 01904 464050 or check www.facebook.com/gatehousecoffee). Remember there is an upstairs worth visiting and, though they do not advertise them, the barbican, portcullis and toilet are behind the counter-bar downstairs – so ask. The door to the barbican wall-walk is to the left in the wall behind the counter-bar; the portcullis looks like heavy trellis shelving disappearing behind cupboards at the back of the counter-bar. The toilet – though not itself medieval! – is attractively fitted into medieval walling at the right. These rooms were probably ruined by parliamentary cannon bombardment in 1644 and then repaired by 1648 using money that parliament confiscated from royalist supporters (see photographs on page 113).

Barbican wall-walk (off-trail extra)

Stories: The Civil War

The last time that the Walls were attacked was also the only time that York has been besieged, with armies circling the city. This was in 1644 during the English Civil War between forces loyal to the King and those supporting a parliament which wanted to limit the King's powers.

The Walls and bars were three or four hundred years old at this time and gunpowder and large cannon had made them much less of a protection than they had been in the Middle Ages. Despite this, the King moved an army into York, personally inspected the old defences and arranged for them to be strengthened. Parliament's supporters in York and Yorkshire created their own army and in the summer of 1644 they were outside the Walmgate section of the Walls. They were joined by a Scottish army on the south side of the city as well as another parliamentarian army on the north side.

A large cannon, firing 25 kilogram cannonballs, was dragged to Heslington Hill outside the city, 200 metres east of Walmgate Bar. It exchanged fire with cannon mounted on Clifford's Tower, half a kilometre west of the Bar. St Sampson's, a church in the centre of York, was hit but it is said that Lord Fairfax, who commanded the Yorkshire parliamentarians, threatened death to anyone who damaged the Minster with their fire.

Walmgate Bar was badly damaged by cannon fire but it also came under secret attack from below ground. Parliamentarian forces were digging a tunnel, probably planned to go under the bar itself, to be filled with gun powder and blown up so that the bar fell in ruins. Over on the other side of York, St Mary's Tower lost a wall this way (and was then stormed by attacking troops who were only forced back by fierce hand-to-hand fighting). Perhaps the defenders were suspicious that something like this was planned; in any case they captured a parliamentarian soldier, questioned him and learned that the undermining at Walmgate Bar was nearly complete. The defenders quickly dug a shallow tunnel of their own to cross above the route of the attackers' tunnel, then they flooded their shallow tunnel with water. This flooded the attackers' tunnel too, so that it had to be abandoned.

The Walls were actively defended like this until Prince Rupert arrived with a Royalist army to relieve York. There followed a large battle just west of the city, on Marston Moor. The Royalists were defeated in this battle and so gave up hopes of being able to hold York – they negotiated a surrender that allowed the Royalist soldiers to leave York with their weapons and promised that many of the parliamentarian troops who would take their place would be Yorkshiremen.

The parliamentarians thought they needed to be able to defend York so they quickly repaired the Walls but in fact what the King and Prince Rupert feared would happen did happen: the loss of York led quickly to the loss of the north of England and that led to the loss of the Civil War. King Charles I kept scheming for victory even when he was imprisoned and so he was executed. For eleven years England was ruled without a king.

MAP OF TRAIL PARTS 8-10

The South Corner:
Walmgate Bar to
Micklegate Bar

N ←——+——

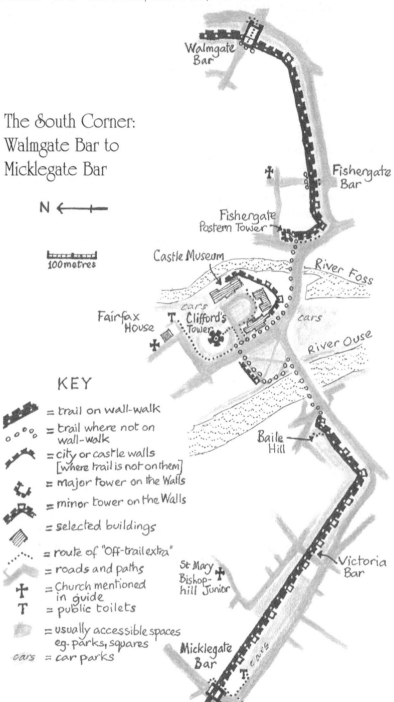

Walmgate
Bar

Fishergate
Bar

Fishergate
Postern Tower

Castle Museum

River Foss

Fairfax
House

T. Clifford's
Tower

cars

cars

River Ouse

Baile
Hill

Victoria
Bar

St Mary
Bishop-
hill Junior

Micklegate
Bar

KEY

= trail on wall-walk

o o o o = trail where not on
            wall-walk

= city or castle walls
   [where trail is not on them]

= major tower on the Walls

= minor tower on the Walls

= selected buildings

······ = route of "off-trail extra"

= roads and paths

✝ = Church mentioned
     in guide

T = public toilets

= usually accessible spaces
   eg. parks, squares

cars = car parks

50

THE TRAIL: 8. SOUTH CORNER PART 1

Basics

Part one of this corner starts with the steps going up to the Walls on the south side of Walmgate Bar and ends where the Walls end at Fishergate Postern Tower.

The first interval tower has excellent views, a bench and broad, low embrasures you can sit in. Looking back there are the Walls, the bar with its barbican and, further away and to the left, a brick side of the low, rebuilt tower of St Margaret's church tower, Victorian Rowntree Wharf with its brick tower, and the Minster. (More details are in "Views" below). This section of Walls has no railings but the drop is generally very low on the inside.

You are forced off the Walls just to cross a little road at Fishergate Bar. This bar was so badly damaged in an attack in 1489 that it was left bricked up for 340 years. Some stones in the archway are pink from when the bar was torched in this attack (details in "Off-trail extra").

Looking forward when the Walls turn west: a modern pub echoes the medieval towers around it

Back on the Walls you soon turn right at a rectangular corner tower. At this corner there is an interesting view and a bench. Ahead of you is Fishergate Postern Tower, guarding a small entrance at the end of this bit of wall-walk. It was also guarding the dam on the River Foss, where the dual carriageway road now turns left and crosses the river.

The dam was to flood the castle's moats; these have all now been filled in, but from here you can see what remains of the castle wall and, half-hidden behind it, Clifford's Tower which was the castle's keep. Between the keep and the castle wall is the 1705 prison, now part of the Castle Museum. Some say that the new pub/hotel in the middle of this view has spoilt it but architects have tried hard to make the building fit in.

This part of the trail ends with the small, late medieval gateway that is to your left as you get to the bottom of the steps at Fishergate Postern Tower. This is the only postern (secondary) gate left in the city walls because, when they were no longer thought of as conveniently easy to block up for defence, these small gates were seen as inconveniently blocking traffic.

Fishergate Postern beside its protective tower

THE TRAIL: 8. SOUTH CORNER PART 1

Details

The wall-walk has just simple battlements for a while, then musket loops probably made for the Civil War. They are currently of a height useful to a kneeling soldier. This length of wall is one of the few for which there are details of the medieval contract to build it. It was relatively late, in 1345, that the corporation agreed the contract. As well as money, the builder was to receive a robe each year and could keep anything of value he found when digging the foundations.

The sharp change of direction of the Walls at the rectangular corner tower was probably to help defend the dam across the Foss. If the dam had been broken by attackers this would have drained the defensive moats in this area (one of the few areas where we are sure the Walls had water in its moat) and eventually would have drained much of the water from the marshy lake that was used for defence further upstream.

As you approach Fishergate Postern Tower, which was built to replace an earlier tower in about 1500, look how the window just below its roof has been made out of an embrasure in the battlements that were once there. This adaptation is much clearer from the outer side of the tower (on your left) where there are three ex-embrasures and a single slit window; the small postern gate you are coming to could be defended from fire from these battlements, the slit window and the Walls. As you go through the postern gateway you can see it had a portcullis (from the deep grooves on both sides of the gateway) as well as a hinged door. It is just possible that the tower will be open to visitors when you

The Walls and Fishergate Postern Tower (David Patrick)

get to it – the Friends of York Walls do open it sometimes (normally for free entry) and plan to do so more.

Views

From the first interval tower: the basics of the views here are given on page 51 but, closer than the Minster, you can also see other medieval church towers – for example the lantern tower of All Saints, Pavement and, much closer and amongst the houses, that of St Denys.

Looking outside the Walls there's a neat, redbrick, early Victorian flax factory, now converted into flats. The trees and buildings behind and to its right suggest the rising ground of Lamel Hill where cannon were based to fire on York during the Civil War. Close behind the factory there is the Victorian spire of a church on another cannon site.

Below you and to the right you see wide roads, a fairly gently sloped rampart and a building site/new build – there was room for this because for most of the last two centuries this area was a large cattle market.

From Fishergate Bar: look towards the city, past the Phoenix pub (not named after the bar which was reborn from the fires of 1489, but for an iron foundry that was once close) and about 100 metres away there's the end of a Victorian church on the right of the road. Opposite it, on the left of the road, is an older churchyard – this is where Dick Turpin, highwayman and folk hero is buried.

Off-trail extras: Fishergate Bar

When you get to the pavement at Fishergate Bar turn left, watch out for passing bikes and go to the inner part of the main archway. Notice the reddened and cracked stones there, most obviously on the left, 3-4 courses of stone from the ground, just before the archway itself. Some magnesian limestone seems to react this way to extreme heat and it is thought that the bar was burned down in 1489. The bar had probably been rebuilt only 50 years earlier and at that time was a major gateway into the city. A little further on you can see the deep grooves its portcullis would have slid in.

Go further still and look back at the outside of the arch – there is carving above it to commemorate repairs to the Walls you have just walked along, repairs completed at the expense of Lord Mayor William Todd in 1487. An attack on Bootham Bar was defeated in the same year and the Mayor was knighted as a result. Both attacks were essentially against the rule of Henry VII, and the attack that destroyed this bar began as a protest against a new tax he was imposing. The corporation decided to save money on repairs and on paying someone to man the bar by simply bricking up the gateway.

The foot tunnels you can see on either side of the main gateway are probably late medieval and can remind us of when some other gates into York were once short tunnels through the earth ramparts; it was in late Georgian and Victorian times that the ramparts were cut back from the sides of the bars and extra stone arches built for cars or pedestrians or both. It is possible to spot masons' marks in both tunnels – for example if you go back into the walled city through the right hand tunnel you can find a three-line arrow head on your right. It is on the stone that is four in and four up (and also on the stone that is above and to the left of this stone). The shaping of this stone (and others) with a claw chisel is also still clear in these tunnels, where there has been little weathering of stones that were probably cut almost 600 years ago.

Chisel marks and a mason's mark at Fishergate Bar (off-trail extra)

Stories: Plague

The Walls were built to defend York from highly visible enemies but the corporation also tried to use them as a defence against a deadly enemy that could not be seen except through the damage it did. In the Middle Ages people did not understand the causes of the illnesses that suddenly spread through the population; in fact even 300 years after medieval times, the people of mid-Victorian England still had epidemics of killer diseases they didn't understand. There was still talk then of "bad air" and at that time some thought it would be healthier to get rid of the Walls to improve the flow of air into the city. But in medieval times, and for two hundred years afterwards, the corporation tried to use the Walls to keep out the people and the goods they thought might be carrying a plague.

If there was known to be plague in the country the keepers of the bars and posterns were reinforced and instructed to keep out goods (especially cloth) and people that had come from places known to have the disease. People who were likely to have wandered through many places and who had no clear business in the city were also to be kept out – including, rather sadly, "women who pretend that they are the wives of soldiers".

There are records of people being punished for helping tradesmen climb over the Walls with their goods, or for making arrangements to let people through the gates by night. Perhaps because the rules were broken, national plagues usually got into York; in the 1604 plague York lost almost a third of its population. Possibly because of this experience, when plague returned to the country in 1631 the Lord President of the Council of the North, based at the King's Manor, just outside the Walls, took control of the city's defences. Posterns like Fishergate Postern were kept locked and the Walls were patrolled. At Walmgate Bar milkmaids handed their cows over to a herdsman, who took them to the common pastures to graze and then brought them back to the city for milking. Plague still got into the city but the death rate was not so high; if plague could be kept out for a while this was useful, as plagues tended to die out when winter came.

In 1631 the first victims in the city were taken to special "pest-houses" built in the fields outside the city walls – people who got ill outside the Walls were imprisoned in their own homes. A watchman was put outside their homes – there were, for instance, four watchmen on the road leading from Walmgate Bar. A saying from the time about plagues was "the rich fly, the poor die" and there are records showing that during some plagues the corporation found it difficult to continue to govern the city because so few of the city elite actually stayed. The Lord President seems to have stayed at his post, living just outside the walled city where the plague seems to have been worse. Both his wife and son died in the epidemic. His coat of arms is carved on a building he added to the King's Manor (see pages 96-8). He was Thomas Wentworth, the last Lord President of the Council of the North.

THE TRAIL: 9. SOUTH CORNER PART 2

Basics

This part of the trail is off the Walls. It crosses the River Foss and then the River Ouse, and runs beside the castle which was built between the two rivers. Go through the small arch by Fishergate Postern Tower and cross the road that's immediately in front of you – the trail markers suggest you go a few metres left along the pavement to use the island in the road. Then go along the right hand pavement of the busy dual carriageway road and you are soon on the bridge over the Foss. There's a good view behind you of the Walls and its towers. As you walk on you will see what is left of the main castle walls on your right. This was the south wall of the castle; in front of it there's what is left of the drawbridge pit.

Continue along the pavement until a quiet road crosses your path; at this point, slightly to your right, on the top of its steep man-made hill is Clifford's Tower. This was the castle's keep and look-out post. The man-made hill dates from 1068 when William the Conqueror came to York and realised it needed a castle, and 500 occupying soldiers, to keep the city under his control. When his first castle, made of wood, was destroyed within the year in spite of its hill and moat, he revisited, rebuilt and realised that it would need two castles to keep York conquered. The stone castle and its keep were built about the same time as the Walls of the city and are part of the defences that ring the city.

The drawbridge pit in front of the castle walls

Cross the quiet road in front of you (it leads to the steps up to Clifford's Tower and to the Castle Museum with its cafe) and then use the pelican crossing to cross the road to your left. Carry on walking in the same direction, through the gardens to the banks of the River Ouse (unless the river is in flood, in which case simply stay on the pavement and go left then over the next bridge). Once you are in the gardens the Walls start on your right – but look strangely low as the ground here has been raised to lessen flooding. The trail goes straight on to the banks of the Ouse where Davy Tower has been made into a house. Once the river could be sealed off as a route of attack by a chain that ran from this tower to another that existed at the time on the other bank. The trail now turns left along the bank of the Ouse and then left up steps to the near side of the road which crosses the Ouse. These gardens have long been common land, once used for archery practice, washing and drying clothes and starting processions.

Go across the bridge: Hull and the sea are 50 miles downstream, and this route made York an important naval trading city until sea-going boats got bigger at the end of the Middle Ages. The trail markers lead you straight on across the relatively quiet road to where the Walls start again and part 3 of this corner of the Walls begins.

Davy Tower made into a house

Details

Most details about this part of the east corner are given in the "Views" and "Stories" below but if immediately after crossing the road at the start of this part of the trail you go a few metres right to a tree, you can look back at Fishergate Postern Tower. You can see its main outer wall with a single slit window and battlements that have been converted into a row of three windows under its roof. You can also see the plinth at the bottom of this wall get lower in steps as it goes left; the ground level probably dropped away there and the River Foss came up against this left corner of the tower. You can just see a medieval toilet sticking out from the left of the tower, so waste from it could drop straight into the river.

Much later, when you have turned away from Clifford's Tower, as soon as you have crossed the pelican crossing and while you are still on the pavement, look for a gate a few metres to your right; it leads to a little lane that seems to be called Tower Place. If you look down this lane you see the inside of the Walls and a narrow stone ledge from which to defend them.

Looking back to Fishergate Postern Tower

The trail goes into the gardens on the outside of the Walls where there was once a ditch, as well as a generally lower ground level. There is an information board at this point and some flood levels are marked. Later in your route through Tower Gardens more information is written on oval metal plates mounted on low concrete pillars.

There is a small tower built into the bridge but with its base in Tower Gardens. This usually has a summer season as a café but originally housed the winding mechanism that allowed the near section of this bridge to be raised to let tall ships through. This is a mid-Victorian bridge which could be raised for the first hundred years of its life.

Views

From the bridge over the Foss and after: see "Basics", but there's more to be said about the south wall of the castle: the newer-looking stonework behind the drawbridge pit was the site of one of the two main gates of the castle but this gate was blocked by royalist forces in the Civil War when they strengthened York's defences. In the right foreground of your view there's a watermill, which is a reminder that there were mills close to here using the water that flowed by the great dam. However this particular mill was moved here to be an exhibition in the Castle Museum (see "Off-trail extra: 4" on page 63).

As you walk on and turn gently right you come close to a round tower in the castle walls which has has lost its battlements at the top of its walls. At their bottom the walls splay out, partly so that rocks dropped from the walls would bounce or roll out at attackers. Some other towers you'll see also have this "batter".

Soon the castle walls stop and you see the back of York's main criminal court. It was mainly built around 1770 and for the first half of the 19th century there were public hangings in front of where the castle walls meet the court. The castle walls here enclose York's "Debtors' Prison", so called because only those imprisoned for debt stayed a long time in the prison; those convicted of crimes were mainly hanged or transported to prison colonies.

A few metres after crossing the quiet road by Clifford's Tower: you might be able to see cracks running down the tower's walls – for example one goes through a window which has been half closed-up by the repair – and how the walls of the gatehouse to the right seem to lean out. You should expect cracks and leaning (or worse) if you put stone walls on a hill built for a wooden castle. We know some of the cracks appeared and were mended soon after the stone tower was built, especially when floods weakened the hill. For some more information see the story "The Stone Stealer" on page 66.

Up the main road on your left you can see grand red-brick Victorian buildings, including the flamboyant, clock-towered, magistrates' court. The council created this road in Victorian times to break through a set of "Water Lanes" leading down to the river – the lanes were thought to be a home to crime and disease.

From the banks of the Ouse: trees may obscure the views but somewhere in the gardens you can usually can find good views of Clifford's Tower.

In the opposite direction, on the opposite bank of the river, you can usually see that there is another hill to match that of Clifford's Tower. It has been tree-covered since Georgian times. It is easier to see that amongst the modern flats and a hotel there are warehouses and mill buildings, which are a reminder that York was an important trading centre, connected to the sea by the Ouse which was tidal until mid-Georgian times.

From the bridge over the Ouse: looking ahead and to your right, you can see these warehouse buildings along with quays, originally for the landing of goods on both sides of the river.

Clifford's Tower (from a little off-trail, in Tower Gardens)

Off-trail extras: 1. Masons' marks

Turn left along the pavement at the very start of this part of the trail (as you stand beside Fishergate Postern Tower instead of crossing the road in front of you). This takes you along one of the few sections of the Walls where most people can spot masons' marks from the pavement. Several masons' marks have been recorded here and one is easy to point out: about halfway to the square corner tower ahead of you the Walls change direction slightly; you can see the vertical line in the stones where this happens. The mason's mark is on the first stone past this change of direction, about two metres up. To be exact, there is a plinth which sticks out a little along the bottom of the Walls and the mark is four courses above this plinth. It is in the form of two linked V shapes pointing left. The marks seem to stop when you reach the rectangular corner tower. There is more about masons' marks in the "Stone and Stonework" section on page 104.

Off-trail extras: 2. Pub

When you cross the road at the very start of this part of the trail you are outside a recently built pub, "The Postern Gate". It is run by Wetherspoons, so it has fairly cheap food and a good range of drinks. There is wheelchair access to the pub, its toilets and a terrace looking out onto the River Foss and castle walls. It is in a modern building that in this author's opinion fits in very well with its medieval neighbours but it has been criticised for blocking out views of the Minster.

Off-trail extras: 3. Clifford's Tower

The tower has its own wall-walk around the top with very extensive views, perhaps the best in York. This walk usually causes mild problems for people with a medium fear of heights (more problems than the Walls usually cause, though the tower's wall-walk has railings on both

The Eye of York from high on Clifford's Tower (David Patrick, off-trail extra)

sides). The tower is basically a safe and interesting 13th century ruin in the care of English Heritage. They charge for entry but are happy for you to climb the steps up its Norman hill without paying. They are very unhappy however if people walk on the grass and earth of the hill. The stone plaque at the bottom of its steps is explained by "The Saddest Story" on page 65. Even without going up the steps you can probably see that the roofed gatehouse at the top of the steps doesn't match the main walls of the tower; looked at from above, it's like a stubby stem to the four-leafed clover of the main tower. This gatehouse was mostly built in the 1640s to prepare for the Civil War and cannon fire from outside the city. The two coats of arms, now rather weathered, were also carved at this time; the top one is the King's.

Off-trail extras: 4. Museums and more

This is a very attractive extra even if you don't wish to go into the museum. The quiet road you cross before reaching Clifford's Tower's hill takes you 60 metres to a flat green space known as "the Eye of York". It was where non-secret voting took place to decide who should represent Yorkshire in parliament (in late Georgian times electing William Wilberforce who led the anti-slavery movement to success). Three buildings face the Eye, the one you have passed is still the highest criminal court in York built for this role almost 250 years ago. You can see a figure with scales of fairness and a spear of punishment on its roof. Opposite the crown court is its twin, built as a women's prison. Between the twins is an earlier building, the Debtors' Prison of 1705. These last two buildings now house the Castle Museum. It is mainly a museum of everyday things from the past, but it also features bits of the prison and medieval castle. On entering, and before you have to pay for entry, are its café, bookshop and toilets.

Magistrates' Court, Clifford's Tower and Castlegate from the Eye of York (off-trail extra)

Off-trail extras: 5. Toilets (ancient and modern), Fairfax House and Jorvik

When the trail turns away from Clifford's Tower at the pelican crossing leave the trail by walking clockwise around the tower, staying on the pavement or on the grass. When the pavement ends with car park entrances there are public toilets 50 metres straight in front of you. An island between the entrances has a finger post and map, and to your left here is Castlegate with a fine Georgian house, Fairfax House, that is open to visitors. Beyond this is St. Mary's, a spired medieval church, which often hosts free art exhibitions and installations. Immediately behind St Mary's is Coppergate, containing the world-famous Jorvik – York's Viking museum.

This route also allows you to see something of Clifford Tower's medieval toilets: in the middle of your walk around the tower, look up at its lower walls for a vertical, rounded stone shoot between two, angled vertical supports for the "garde-robe" turret.

Clifford's Tower showing its garde-robe shoot (off-trail extra)

This shoot took the waste from the first floor toilet of the tower down to the top of the hill – where it would be an added discouragement to anyone attacking the tower! That is unless they chose to try a sneak attack up the shoot – at least one medieval castle is said to have been successfully attacked this way!

Stories: 1. The saddest story

More than 800 years ago, in 1190, something deeply sad happened on the hill where Clifford's Tower now stands. It is difficult to be sure about the details because it happened so long ago and different writers from the time disagree on the details, but the truth is something like this:

There was a community of Jews living in York, and some other cities, but everyone else in the country was officially Christian. The Christians were what we'd call today Roman Catholic Christian because they accepted the pope in Rome as the head of their Church. The pope had asked Christians to go on a military crusade to put Jerusalem under Christian control (although to most of the Muslims who lived in and around Jerusalem, of course, this was a military invasion of their lands) – and the new king of England was getting ready to go on this Crusade. A rumour began that the new crusader-king no longer wanted to protect the non-Christian Jews of England, some even said you didn't have to go abroad to find enemies of Christianity to kill. There were a lot of anti-Jewish attacks at this time; Jews were injured, killed or forced to convert to Christianity – sometimes all three.

The attack in York was a particularly bad one and the Jews of York went to the King's Tower at the top of its hill for protection. They were let in and prepared to defend themselves but were surrounded by a large crowd of armed knights and ordinary people. After holding out against the crowd for a while most of them decided to choose their own death rather than fall into the hands of their attackers; they probably organised in families so that everyone who agreed had their throat slit and died quickly. Some probably didn't agree to this, but it seems that any survivors of the mass suicide were killed by the attackers – and sometime during all this the wooden tower on the hill was burnt down. Probably about 150 men, women and children were killed, the whole Jewish community in York.

This sounds like a story of religious hatred but there's a complication. At that time Jews were not allowed to join the trade guilds so one of the few ways they could earn money was by lending it and charging interest. Money lenders are seen as very useful when you want to borrow money from them – but as evil when they want their interest paid or their money back. It seems that the attack in York was started by people who owed money to local Jews and it also seems that as soon as the Jews were dead the mob ran to the Minster – not for a Christian service to celebrate the death of the unbelievers but so they could break into the Minster chests where records of debts were kept and burn these records.

There's a post-script to this story: in late March, which is when the massacre happened, these slopes are covered with flowering daffodils and many of them were planted in the 1990s as a memorial to the Jews who died here. Daffodils were chosen because they are yellow and around the trumpet is a ruff of six petals, which looks a little like the star of David, associated with Judaism.

Clifford's Tower at daffodil time

Stories: 2. The Stone Stealer

Today sociologists would call it a "white collar crime"; I imagine this as a frilly white Elizabethan ruff crime. A gaoler decided to take advantage of the fact that he was in charge of York Castle and he turned thief. Towards the end of Queen Elizabeth I's time, rather more than 400 years ago when the stone tower had been standing for 350 years, Clifford's Tower was just the most striking part of York Castle. This castle had tall walls all round it, but they were falling into disrepair – literally dilapidated, the stones were getting loose and falling out. The main use of the castle was as a prison and an enterprising man called Robert Redhead was put in charge of it. This was a royal appointment, nothing to do with York's Lord Mayor or corporation but we know from their records that citizens started to notice something strange about what they thought of as "their" Clifford's Tower; it was shrinking! It seems that the gaoler was slowly dismantling it. Some say he was burning the stone to make lime which could be sold, others that he was using the stone to build a cock-pit in town – a place where cockerels were brought to fight and where people could watch and bet on the outcome of the fight. The corporation complained to the Queen and eventually Redhead was stopped but not before the level of the wall-walk and the battlements above them had been lowered by half a metre or more.

Clifford's Tower gargoyle (off-trail extra)

There's evidence you can see of this lowering. If you look at the tower from the place suggested in "Views" then you can see, at the top of the tower on your left, a stone spout sticking out – this is actually a very weathered gargoyle. Water drained off the wall-walk and came gurgling through the mouth of this gargoyle – but you may be able to see that this spout is now some way above the level of today's wall-walk behind it. You can also see, on what was a tall parapet, the very bottom of slit windows to fire arrows through, but most of the stonework around the windows has gone. The clearest one of these slit window bottoms is just to the right of the right hand end of the thicker safety rail; it looks a little like the socket for a dove-tail joint.

Signs of stolen stones at Clifford's Tower

THE TRAIL: 10. SOUTH CORNER PART 3

Basics

This part of the trail is on the wall-walk. It starts by going up some Victorian steps and through a Victorian tower in order to climb a flat-topped hill that was made for one of William the Conqueror's wooden "motte and bailey" castles about 950 years ago.

The motte was the hill for the castle keep; the bailey was the defended space next to it. After climbing almost to the top of the motte the Walls run on two sides of the bailey, built on mounds that the Normans had wooden walls on. Soon after leaving the bailey mounds, the wall-walk goes over the top of an arch called Victoria Bar, in honour of the new Queen at the time when it was cut through the ramparts and Walls. Oddly, the cutting showed there had been a medieval gate here.

Soon there is a sign set into the paving of the wall-walk to tell you to look slightly to your right to see the oldest church tower in York. It was built of Roman stone some years before the Norman Conquest, about 100 metres from the ramparts which were later to carry the Walls. The outer ramparts here have the most varied wild flowers of anywhere on the ramparts. It is probable that the ramparts from now on contain the remains of the walls that the Romans built around the important civilian town that grew up across the river from their legionary fort. This south corner of the trail ends at Micklegate Bar.

The Walls south of Baile Hill (David Patrick)

THE TRAIL: 10. SOUTH CORNER PART 3

Details

The first little bit of the Walls replaces a medieval wall that ran down to a tower at the river's edge and included a postern gate and a tower to guard it. This was the first bit of wall that the corporation knocked down – it resulted in the corporation being successfully sued by the archbishop.

Archbishops have a long history of being in charge of this area of the Walls – in the early Middle Ages they were responsible for the defence of the castle here and there were conflicts with the citizens when this was one of the last sections of the Walls not yet built in stone. In the 1320s the danger from Scotland increased and Archbishop Melton arranged for the castle bailey's wooden walls to be replaced by stone ones. It is thought he pulled masons off their work building the Minster in order to get the work here done fast. Evidence that this happened comes from reports that the masons' marks here seem to match some found in the Minster – the only mark I have found that can be seen from the trail is in the bottom course of stones of the parapet of the first interval tower after the steps; it is on the fourth stone from the right and it looks like a triangle with two of its sides extended at one corner (see the photograph on page 105).

The archbishop's experiences in the disasterous battle of Myton in 1319 (see the Story on page 12) may have made him eager to strengthen the walls here.

The corner tower has a stylised map set into its paving (see the photograph on page 111). It could be a puzzle but it's to remind you that if you look back you can see the motte of one of William the Conqueror's castles – and that the motte of the other is on the other side of the Ouse, with its current tower, Clifford's Tower, sometimes visible from this point.

This corner tower is intriguingly called Bitchdaughter Tower; why it has this name remains a puzzle. If you look over its battlements you can see its walls splay out at the base either for structural strength or to deflect heavy rocks and other items which could be dropped on attackers. Much of its stonework may be of the Civil War period, as records suggests a tower here slipped away from the Walls and had its stone taken and used for repairing York bridge in 1566.

There is another small puzzle 50 metres past the next tower – it seems to be a gaming board roughly cut into the paving.

On the outer ramparts there is a biggish patch of an interesting wild flower that may have been there since it was brought to York by the Romans. They are called alexanders (for more information and a photograph see the Appendix, page 107, on "Flowers of the Walls and Ramparts"). To find it, look out for a tree very close to the Walls quite a way past Victoria Bar and only about 100 metres short of Micklegate Bar, then look down the outer ramparts to the base of the lowest trees in the group. The darkish green, fairly glossy leaves come up in February and it flowers yellow in spring.

Bitchdaugher Tower from the south (David Patrick)

Views

From the wall-walk above Victoria Bar: in gaps between the trees you have a clear but distant view of the Minster at the opposite side of the walled city so you get a good impression of the size of old York, perhaps to match the impression your feet are giving you! To the left of the Minster and much closer to you is the tower of St Mary's, Bishophill Junior. The spire to the right of the Minster is the medieval church of St Mary's, Castlegate (Castlegate, unsurprisingly, runs from the city centre to Clifford's Tower). Just across the road from you is a Victorian Methodist chapel; the housing just inside the Walls throughout this part is Victorian.

From the next interval tower: this tower has the paving marker for the view of St Mary's, Bishophill Junior, referred to in "Basics", as having the oldest church tower in York.

Baile Hill from Bitchdaughter Tower (David Patrick)

If you look outside the Walls you can see, about a kilometre away to your left, what was once York's second-biggest sweet factory, Terry's, with its clock tower. The business was bought by a multinational company who kept the brand name but ended manufacturing in York. To the right, and much closer to you, is a late Victorian school looking a little like a palace-castle in a Disney cartoon. It is pleasing to imagine that its architect, like Disney, wished to delight children; after all it was built when the law had just been changed to rescue those under eleven from employment and sociologists say the Victorians invented childhood, by developing the idea that children should be treated as special. Eventually you can see this palace of childhood quite well at the end of a road leading to the Walls. It is about 200 metres away.

Off-trail extras: 1. Baile Hill

This extra adds little except, perhaps, for some children who find walking along a paved wall-walk a bit dull. Please note you need to judge for yourself what is safe for you and what will not damage the Walls or the old man-made hill – but I don't think that everyone needs to avoid the following mild temptation.

When you get to the top of the steps at the start of this part of the trail it is possible to use the end of the railings on your right to clamber down off the walls onto the upper slopes of the Norman motte on your right. You can then walk up the slope to the flat top that once held a wooden tower to look out over the city, the river and the land around, looking for danger to York – or danger from York because the Norman conquerors were not popular with local people. Your best route back is the one you have taken to get here.

Baile Hill from the east (David Patrick)

Off-trail extras: 2. Victoria Bar

There are steps down from the wall-walk at Victoria Bar so you may wish to use these to have a look at the bar at ground level. You are likely to find this a disappointment but there is an information board here about the bar and for a few hundred metres further west there is a pleasant green space beside the inner ramparts with a small children's play-park at the end.

Stories: Money and the hidden gate

In York's records about its Walls there are all sorts of snippets of information and all sorts of gaps in the information too. For example there are records of the taxes that were paid at the gates of York on goods brought in to be sold in the city's markets. In 1226 there was a charge of 1 penny for a loaded cart, though only a halfpenny if it was loaded in Yorkshire, and a halfpenny for each cow or horse. A halfpenny then was the daily pay for an unskilled female labourer. The Walls and bars made it fairly easy to collect this tax and some say this provided an important extra reason for having the Walls. The problem of bypassing the Walls and entering by river instead was solved by having chains slung across the river – a loaded boat was charged four pennies to enter York.

These taxes were called "murage" because they were meant to be spent on the Walls by the "muremaster" whose unpaid job it was to inspect the Walls and arrange for necessary repairs. We have some records of the people who were elected to be muremasters. Historians think they have evidence that few willingly stood for election so first it was made something you had to have done if you wanted to become Lord Mayor and then the work was handed over to someone with a marvellous job title, "the Common Husband". (Currently it's done by the CYC Asset Engineer). There are also old records that mention a gateway called Lounelith – but then all mention of this gateway ceases.

Lounelith is said to mean "secluded gate" and I like to think of it as "the lonely gate". Sadly, if a gate is lonely it is not going to have many people pressing to have it kept in good repair and if a muremaster should think that repairs, and the pay of the gatekeeper, are going to cost more than the murage collected at that little-used gate, then he'll want it closed up rather than repaired. Whether this is what happened, or whether the Lord Mayor and wardens decided they wanted fewer gates to guard at some time of danger, we will probably never know. It was thought that we'd never even know where the lonely gate was but then in 1838 a busy businessman, George Hudson, became Lord Mayor of York; for more about him see section 12's Story "The Railway King" on page 85. He organised a collection to finance the building of a new gate through the Walls, which he thought would be busy because there was new housing both inside and outside the Walls at the point he had in mind. The collection was successful, the Walls were dismantled at the chosen place and the ramparts were dug away for the building of the new arch. However a strange discovery was made: the ramparts were not just medieval wall foundations, earth and Roman walls, they also seemed to contain an old gateway blocked with large stones, laid on edge so as to fill the gateway as thinly and quickly as possible. Historians think that the lonely gate had been found, though the new gateway on its site was named Victoria Bar, after the new Queen. I don't know if for a while it became a popular and far-from-lonely gate but now it is again a rather quiet, secluded and, perhaps, lonely gate.

Victoria Bar

MAP OF TRAIL PARTS 11-13

The West Corner:
Micklegate Bar to Bootham Bar

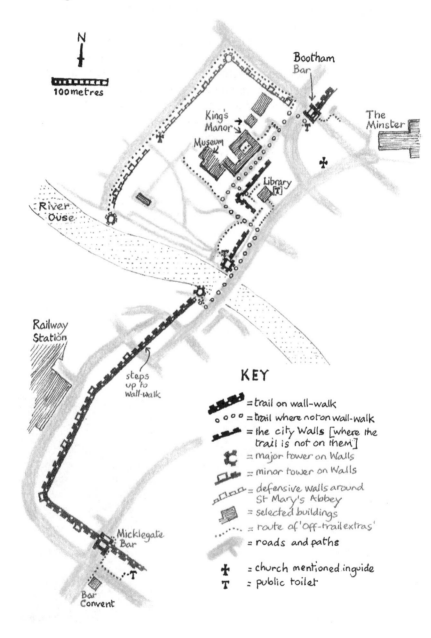

N

100 metres

Bootham
Bar

King's
Manor

Museum

The
Minster

Library

River
Ouse

Railway
Station

steps
up to
Wall-walk

Micklegate
Bar

Bar
Convent

KEY

= trail on wall-walk

o o o o = trail where not on wall-walk

= the city Walls [where the
trail is not on them]

= major tower on Walls

= minor tower on Walls

= defensive walls around
St Mary's Abbey

= selected buildings

= route of 'off-trail extras'

= roads and paths

✝ = church mentioned in guide

T = public toilet

THE TRAIL: 11. MICKLEGATE BAR

Basics

If you are really short of time and are doing the basic trail then stay on the wall-walk as it goes through this bar. After all, the trail takes you to the front of Bootham Bar, the back of Walmgate Bar and some of the arched passages of Monk Bar and Walmgate Bar. However some would say that you will be missing most of the principal bar of York. This is called the principal bar because it guards the main road south which means it is the place where monarchs are greeted and where the heads of people these past monarchs called traitors were mounted. Notice the stone figures on the battlements as you approach and as you leave the bar along the wall-walk – this is probably where the heads would have been spiked. The last ones belonged to supporters of Bonnie Prince Charlie in 1745. He brought a Scottish army further into England than York and scared York people into hurried repairs of the Walls but then retreated back to Scotland and was defeated.

Approaching Micklegate Bar (David Patrick)

THE TRAIL: 11. MICKLEGATE BAR

Details

In Royal greetings here the ceremony involves a loyal speech of welcome to the monarch, and the city's sword-bearer presenting and reversing his ceremonial sword. It is said that King Richard II gave the city a sword from his side and permission to hold it upright more than 600 years ago. When James I was welcomed 400 years ago, he was politely offered the city's sword (he took it and then returned it). When the present Queen is welcomed, the ceremony involves her being presented with the sword and touching it while she is on the outside of the bar. She only goes through the bar when she has symbolically confirmed that the sword belongs to the city. The sword stands for power in the city – monarchs have used many royal charters to give or sell some of their powers to the city since even before King John's 1212 charter. In spite of its gift having been confirmed, the sword is courteously held point downwards when the monarch is actually in the city. Extras were sometimes added to the ceremony, like music or mechanical displays that used the bar as a firm base for the levers and pulleys – and as something to hang scenery from. Henry VII seems to have been greeted by a crown descending from a heaven, pictured at the top of the bar, onto a red and a white rose while other flowers at the bottom of the bar bowed to the two roses.

The figures on the battlements are modern replacements for ones mentioned as getting attention from craftsmen more than 400 years ago. The back of the bar is also relatively new – 1827 – but the bar is basically a much-renewed 14th century building on top of a Norman archway with a room built above that archway around 1200.

There are further interesting details in "Off-trail extras: 2" opposite.

Views

Some like the view into York down Micklegate, the road that runs through this bar. This view is best seen from the wall-walk as it joins the west edge of the bar, which is to say where you leave the bar if you are following our trail. You can just see a large, typical Georgian building, Micklegate House, on the left side of the road before the road disappears round its gentle bend.

Off-trail extras: 1. Toilets

Go outside the bar on the east side of the bar (if following the trail clockwise this means going down the first steps) and turn left along the pavement. It is about 50 metres to the crossroads and then turning left it is about another 50 metres down the road to the public toilets. They are in a car park that has been built where there was once the moat that circled the Walls. On your way back you see the bar as described immediately below.

Off-trail extras: 2. Front of the bar

Go outside the bar on the east side of the bar, as above, turning left along the pavement. After about 30 metres look back at the front of the bar. You'll see numerous straight and cross shaped arrow-slits in the bar. The two small, studded wood doors led to the wall-walk around a defensive barbican, which was built out from the front of the bar in medieval times to strengthen its defences and pulled down in late Georgian times, partly because some of it had fallen down.

The front of Micklegate Bar (off-trail extra)

Switching from defence to decoration, you'll see a royal coat of arms and the city's gold lions on a red cross. The lowest and most striking coat of arms is of the Lord Mayor responsible for an early restoration of the bar. Some details of the restorations – and of the old decorations that we fortunately lack! – are given on an information board on the right of the bar. The other, more modern, boards are on the other side of the bar on this side of the road, and on a wall by the pavement on the other side of the road. This wall also has the metal map for rubbing which features a child's cheerfully ghoulish illustration of a spiked head (see the photograph on page 80).

As you walk back to the bar, look at its arch and the low parts of the side of the passage immediately behind it – the arch is believed to date from Norman times and the passage is built with some re-used Roman stone including coarse sandstone coffins. A brass trail marker suggests you should also peer down this passage from the city-side of the bar. It would be dangerous to think this marker is suggesting that you go into the passage or cross the road at this point. It is better to go up the steps to the wall-walk on this side of the road.

Off-trail extras: 3. Café and museum

Go outside the bar on the east side of the bar, as in the previous two "Off-trail extras", and walk down to the crossroads. Cross over the road in front of you – the traffic lights have a light for pedestrians – and you are at the Bar Convent. Its cafe is through the main entrance about ten metres further on. It is in a fine Georgian building which also houses the oldest Roman Catholic nunnery in England and a free museum. It has more substantial meals than many cafés, free leaflets and a shop. On your way back you will see the bar as described in "Front of the bar" in the previous off-tail extra.

The Bar Convent and Micklegate Bar (off-trail extra)

Off-trail extras: 4. Museum in the bar

The small museum inside the bar is run by the York Archaeological Trust, a charity that charges for its museums. Its displays are changed from time to time but are well presented and some of them are usually closely linked to the Walls. Going in lets you explore some of the inside of the bar, though in this respect the museum is less impressive than Monk Bar – for example there are only parts of the portcullis left. However entry to the first room and shop is free.

Stories: Heads

When the Walls were being completed the succession of kings seemed particularly simple: Edward I's son became Edward II, and his son became Edward III. By the time of Edward III's great-grandchildren things had become more complicated – one of them, Henry VI, was on the throne and another, Richard, Duke of York, had ruled while Henry was ill and was accepted as his heir, but felt he was being squeezed out of having any power at all by Henry's wife. In Shakespeare's version of the story Richard is captured in battle by Queen Margaret's forces; she puts a paper crown on his head, mocks him, stabs him and orders:

> *Off with his head, and set it on York Gates;*
> *so York may overlook the town of York.*

"York Gates" was Micklegate Bar which, more than the other bars, had a tradition of showing the heads of people who had rebelled against royal power. Some say the other bars were more likely to show off the "quarters" of people who had been "hung, drawn and quartered". Richard's head was probably treated with some preservative and topped with a paper crown. Shakespeare suggested that Henry was shocked by what his wife did, saying:

> *to see this sight, it irks my very soul.*
> *Withhold revenge, dear God! 'tis not my fault,*

Henry was right to fear revenge: Richard of York had adult sons to claim his dukedom, to inherit his claim to kingship and to claim revenge. This was the struggle for the crown which the Victorian's labelled "the Wars of the Roses" because the Duke of York used a white rose as a badge. Shakespeare wrote a scene in a rose garden where lords plucked red or white roses to show which side of the struggle they supported.

Revenge came very quickly to Richard's oldest son, Edward, as in the very next year he won the Battle of Towton, just south of York, a battle often described as the bloodiest ever fought in England. He came out of that battle accepted as King Edward IV, then he came to Micklegate Bar where royalty were traditionally welcomed to the city.

His father's head was still spiked above it. Shakespeare has a servant say it was:

The saddest spectacle that e'er I viewed.

Edward had the head removed and replaced by heads from the Lancastrian, red rose, side of the struggle. The struggle did not fully end until Edward's brother, Richard III, was killed in battle and the winner of the battle was crowned Henry VII. He married Edward's daughter in the Minster, uniting the Houses of York and Lancaster, and took as a badge a red and white rose, the "Tudor rose".

A rubbing of ghoulish artwork on Micklegate Bar's metal map (off-trail extra)

Basics

This corner can begin with the steps on either side of the road on the city side of Micklegate Bar; you turn right at the top of the steps. In this part of the Walls the railway has had a big effect and the views a little later in this section are interesting.

At the corner tower, complete with a bench, the view out of the city gives you an idea of how much it has expanded in the last two centuries and reminds you that railways were the major cause of this expansion in Victorian times. Inside the Walls you will see office buildings; many think they are too big and too close to the Walls. They are used for railway-related work and are next to great arched holes in the Walls that were created to let trains steam into York in the 1840s.

As you walk further the view improves. Outside the Walls you have the later Victorian station and the hotel built next to it but the view that develops and changes in front of you, and inside the Walls till the end of this part of the trail, is much better. You see the Walls arching over two roads built to give city people access to the present station; these walls lead the eye to Lendal Tower and then to the Minster, with the half-spire of St Wilfrid's to the left of the Minster.

Part of the popular view that develops as you walk the Walls towards the Minster

Closest to you on the right is the light coloured mix of buildings that make up the new council offices, which include the previous railway station from the 1840s. Beyond these is an elaborate 1906 railway office building, which is now a hotel. The contrasting, simple, white memorial is to the war dead of the railways. From the top of the last two arches you can see, on the near bank of the river, the conical top of the tiny, medieval, Barker Tower and to the right (and just a little more noticeable!) the Aviva building, also on the river bank, also in local magnesian limestone and often thought to be the best wholly modern building in central York.

The view starts with new council offices developed from old railway buildings

THE TRAIL: 12. WEST CORNER PART 1

Details

You might miss an information board about this section of the trail, it is by the pavement near the most westerly arch at Mickelgate Bar.

The corner tower was rebuilt after being "shot down" by cannon fire from the Scottish army in the Civil War siege. Almost 100 metres after the tower there is a stone sign set in the paving of the wall-walk which rather neatly suggests that ahead of you and to the right is the old railway station – you only see glimpses of this Georgian-style light stone building from the Walls – and that an old signal box is in the opposite direction. You can see a very small old railway building if you lean over the battlements to look at where the ramparts have been dug away completely, but railwaymen today say it's unlikely that this was ever a signal box as it only has good windows on two sides of it.

After another 100 metres there's an interval tower, the third from the corner; from here, until you come to the first arch over a road, you can see that the old city moat has been made into a graveyard. This was done in 1832 when there was a cholera epidemic in York and a sudden need for more space for graves. There was even a plan to use all the remaining moats for graves but this was rejected. Many of the graves here are unmarked but the yew trees, traditional in English graveyards, help to mark this as a burial place.

Towards the end of the wall-walk, starting above the road arches, there are a set of musket loops. Several seem to have been made by blocking up the embrasures of battlements. The loops are of uncertain age because much of the Walls from here back to the Corner tower was taken down and rebuilt in Victorian times to allow the arches to be built. Sections of the rampart were removed at the same time and most were not rebuilt – though the inner ramparts beside the new council offices are probably a rebuild as they have air-raid shelters in them. Roman walls were found each time the ramparts were dug into but they do not seem to have definitely been the defensive walls of the Roman civilian town.

Views

From the first interval tower: look back to the buildings at the cross-roads outside Mickelgate Bar and facing you is the Georgian "Bar Convent". If you think that it doesn't look like a place where nuns lived, taught and worshipped then the architect has been successful; in the 1760s Roman Catholic worship and teaching was not generally tolerated (and did not become clearly legal for about 20 years) so it was done secretly – there is a chapel behind the frontage you can see but when it was built it was described as "a new front wall" to the house.

From the corner tower: the suburbs of York stretch for 3 to 4 kilometres from here. The closest building to you on your left is the Railway Institute – built to replace a pub so that the most convenient place of recreation for railway employees was a place where they'd be encouraged to improve themselves rather than intoxicate themselves. To the right of it and behind there used to be factories for making railway rolling stock, as well as buildings and sidings linked to York's importance as a railway junction. From an older era, although they overlapped, you may be able to see a black-bodied, white-sailed windmill mid-way between the Railway Institute and the glazed ends of the arched roofs of the railway station but a kilometre further away. It was from high ground in this sort of area that Scottish army cannon fired on this tower, almost destroying it in 1644 during the Civil War siege. Inside the Walls here the two big office buildings are appropriately named after two giants of the Victorian railway boom – George Stephenson and George Hudson. Hudson House is the darker one you are yet to walk past, and you can read more about him in "The Railway King" story, opposite.

From the second interval tower past the corner tower: this gives you the best view from the Walls of the present railway station, built in 1877. It was said to have been the largest in the world when it was built, and a flagship station for the North Eastern Railway, so it seems to have been designed to fit in with the Walls by having a modest fore-building of pale brick. It is thought to be the finest Victorian building in York but it is much better appreciated from inside. From this tower you can see the hotel to the right of the station, which was built just after it. This is taller and more decorated than the station but it is also respectfully pale and turned away from the Walls, with its octagonal entrance hall turned to the station and its grand front on the opposite side facing its gardens. Just to the left of the octagonal entrance hall you see the station's only original "end screen", for the canopies arching above the railway lines and platforms. The replacement screens in the rest of the station have squarer, simpler, less attractive glass panels. It is the roof, 250 metres by 75 metres, comprising four curving canopies supported by arches on elaborate pillars, that is usually most admired in the station. In the foreground, by the edge of the ramparts and partly hidden by trees, you see a more modern and modest public transport building: the only bus shelter designed to fit its York context.

York's 1870s railway station and hotel

On the inside of the walls at this point you can see an even more recent transport building, a very grand council bike shelter. This 2012 build is a small part of the council's support of cycling – York is officially Britain's safest cycling city.

Off-trail extras: Café

At the very end of the wall-walk there are benches and the trail turns right to the pavement; if, instead of going to the pavement, you go to the steps to your left you see Barker Tower. It is on the banks of the river – and occasionally surrounded by the river when it floods – about 20 metres away. This medieval tower has a beautiful café called the Perky Peacock, but it is small and without a toilet. Currently it's not open at weekends – see www.facebook.com/theperkypeacock for the latest details. If it is open it will have tables and chairs outside it. The archways through the Walls beside the tower replaced a medieval postern gate which survived until George Hudson needed better access to his railway's coal yards. The archways are still sometimes called North Street Postern.

Stories: The Railway King

Up to the start of Victorian times York had various groups of citizens who had local power in the city and some of these elected a Lord Mayor who, for a year, was something like a local king. Most ordinary people had no clear part in this "corporation" – not even if they were eligible to to vote to elect a member of parliament, which is to say old enough, well enough off and male. When this was changed and

One of Hudson's arches and Barker Tower (housing a tiny cafe)

there were "proper elections" the first result in York was a Lord Mayor who seemed rich enough to give all sorts of treats to the new voters. This was George Hudson, who saw himself as a self-made, successful businessman who brought the railways to York.

A legend grew up that, though he had been happy tailoring and running a successful draper's shop, George decided that the new railways were the opportunity York needed to recover its prosperity, so he worked and argued and risked his own money to "mak all t'railways cum t'York". He was certainly successful for a while; he was Lord Mayor three times, was elected to parliament and was said to have controlled a third of the railways in England. National newspapers named him "the Railway King". In York he organised the building of a railway station inside the Walls and the cutting of four arches through the Walls, two of them to let his trains into the station. Some of the money his companies paid to the council for the privilege of cutting through the Walls and ramparts went to repair Walmgate Bar and its barbican.

Then things seemed to go sour for him; the railways did not seem to be making much money and he was accused of paying dividends to old investors by using money from new investors. He was also accused of bribery and of moving money between his different businesses in mysterious and suspicious ways. People started to pursue him for personal and company debts rather than offer him money to invest.

He was at the point of winning an election campaign to get into parliament again when he was arrested for debt, imprisoned in York's debtors' prison and had to withdraw as candidate. The Conservative Party talked of its candidate having been kidnapped. After a few months friends paid this debt so he was released from prison but he felt he had to exile himself to France to prevent future imprisonment.

In the last years of his life he was said to be living in poverty so a popular collection was made to help him live comfortably. Then, and perhaps just as importantly to him, imprisonment for debt was ended in Britain so he returned to the country shortly before he died in 1871.

Some think that when Charles Dickens wrote Little Dorritt he based his financier Merdle on Hudson, though when Merdle's popular business schemes collapse he chooses suicide – it is one of his investors who goes to the debtors' prison that Dickens is attacking in the novel.

A parliamentary election postcard

York's Debtors' Prison

THE TRAIL: 13. WEST CORNER PART 2

Basics

This part begins where the wall-walk stops and Lendal Bridge starts. When you come off the wall-walk the trail runs straight along the pavement, above and past Barker Tower, over the bridge, past Lendal Tower, past a short section of the Walls you can't walk on, to the main entrance of the Museum Gardens.

The pavement is often too busy for you to enjoy the views but when you have come off the bridge a little way (you continue onwards) try to look past the people in front of you. A rather ugly, yellow-grey-pink, Victorian church half-spire appears towards the end of the road and, thanks to perspective, it soon seems to cheekily look down on the massive, elegantly monochrome Minster.

At the iron gates turn left into the Museum Gardens for the grand finale of the trail. The trail goes along the main path in the garden, keeping right when it forks into two, and on your right behind the lawn is the Multangular Tower with a section of Roman wall leading up to it. These are York's best Roman walls above ground, built of neat, small, pale limestone blocks with a stripe of red tiles running through them. They were built at the corner of the legionary fort, probably at the time when the Emperor Constantius was based here, shortly before he died and his son was declared emperor here (see the Story on page 100).

Multangular Tower, showing the gate to its interior (David Patrick)

But, like many of York's best buildings, the tower doesn't belong to a single time period; its top is a medieval wall which is pierced by tall arrow-slits. Moreover, the Roman wall has a rough repair across its red stripe about three metres from where it joins the tower – this may well be a 1640s repair of cannonball damage done in the Civil War. If so then this small section of the Walls shows work from their three most important times: when Roman soldiers first built them, when medieval masons circled the city with them and when they were last used to defend York.

The main path goes on to a museum but the trail turns right immediately after the Multangular Tower. It then goes right again, up a little path that takes you through a gate in the Walls where you can look at the inside of the tower; you can then retrace your steps as far as the flat ground and turn right, leaving the Museum Gardens by a larger gate. The Walls are on your right here but you can't walk on them. Soon they stop suddenly where the corporation knocked them down to build a new road into York almost 200 years ago but the trail continues into a square with a statue of a man who helped save the rest of the Walls. He is looking at Bootham Bar where the trail began.

A rough repair in the Roman Walls near the Multangular Tower

THE TRAIL: 13. WEST CORNER PART 2

Details

Lendal Bridge is a Victorian replacement for a ferry. It is decorated with England's lions, the city's coat of arms, the Minster's crossed keys and the white rose that became the symbol of Yorkshire in Victorian times. (Although it was a symbol the Duke of York used in the Middle Ages, this dukedom did not give him much power or land in Yorkshire so his symbol was not linked to Yorkshire at this time.)

The tower you are crossing towards is Lendal Tower, which in medieval times roughly matched Barker Tower on the side of the River Ouse you are leaving. There used to be a chain that could be stretched between the two towers to bar entrance to York for those wishing to attack by boat or wishing to trade without paying a tax. Lendal Tower grew because for 200 years from 1631 it was used as a pump house and water tower; water was pumped from the river to be distributed through pipes to paying customers throughout York. The little dark sandstone towers at each end of the bridge on the other side of the road are Victorian, as is the tower which guards the gates to the Museum Gardens.

The gardens themselves, and the museum in them, were created a little before Victorian times with a gift of land from the crown. Henry VIII had taken the land from monks in 1539 – more about this in "Off-trail extras: 3. St. Mary's ruins" on page 94. The gift was to the Yorkshire Philosophical Society, a club of local enthusiasts for knowledge which still advertises its open meetings in the tower by the museum gates.

The entrance to the gardens are in a puzzling gap in the Walls, which reappear on your right as Roman walls – at first these are behind a flower bed. This bed is "planted in depth" in a way suitable for the gardens of a museum – it has plants of the prairies, trees and Roman coffins. The red stripe in the Walls here is probably partly Roman military swagger – the complete walls had two layers of big red tiles, sticking out a little from the pale limestone walls so that their red stripe would be underlined by a line of shadow – and partly for structural strength, as the tower walls are made of two thin walls of shaped limestone blocks and a filling between them of rubble and mortar. These two thin walls are tied together by the layer of red tiles going right through the whole wall.

Just past the Multangular Tower, where the trail branches right off the main path, there is a large flat dark stone with "cup and ring" carvings.

The meaning and exact age of this kind of carving is a mystery but it is thought the oldest in Britain. When you have gone up the short branch of the trail to a view of the inside of the Multangular Tower you'll see the tower walls have the neatly laid inner skin of cut stones but the walls beyond are rough; this is because the Romans had an earth embankment on the inner side of the walls between the towers. Some experts think this walling was built a hundred years before Constantine, a time when the Emperor Severus was based in York. For more about this area see "Off-trail extras: 4" on page 95 or the information board immediately to the left inside the little gate through the Walls.

Cup and ring carvings in the Museum Gardens

When you have left the gardens by the big gate the building on your left is "the King's Manor" – this started as the house of the Abbot of St Mary's (the leader of the monks who once owned the site of the Museum Gardens) but Henry VIII took it and renamed it. It developed as the headquarters of the Council of the North; its Lord President lived here and, in a sense, ruled the north of England for the monarch from the time of Henry VIII until the English Civil War. For more about this building see "Off-trail extras: 5" on page 96.

When you get to the square you'll see one side of it has medieval-looking walls with a tower by an archway – these were built to defend St. Mary's Abbey, the home of the Museum Garden monks. What's left of the city walls at this point is Bootham Bar, on the far side of the road that was built through the bar's barbican and then through the Walls themselves. The monks wanted the walls to defend them against those York people who resented their wealth and power. For more about these walls see "Off-trail extras: 6. St Mary's walls" on page 98.

Views

From the bridge and later: in front of you and to your left, on the bank of the Ouse, are the Museum Gardens and at their left edge (and the water's edge) there is the tower at the end of walls built to defend St Mary's Abbey in the mid 13th century. To your right, rising straight from the river, you may see glimpses of the limestone walls of the Guild Hall, which was medieval but was heavily restored after fire damage in World War Two. However looking straight ahead you can see the church described in "Basics" on page 88. The fact that the odd-looking half-spire is of a Roman Catholic church may explain why it seems to be trying to give the impression that it can look down on the Minster, which ceased to be Roman Catholic at the time of Henry VIII. York has a history of producing assertive Roman Catholics, the most famous being Guy Fawkes, born within 100 metres of this church (but 300 years before it was built and 200 years before any Roman Catholic Church could be built legally in England).

Cheek! St Wilfrid's appears to look down on the Minster

From the grass in front of the Multangular Tower: between the trees as you look in the direction the main path is going you should see the most admired ruins in York, those of St Mary's Abbey church whose limestone frames a row of gothic windows. (For more about this see "Off-trail extras: 3" on page 94). Many of the trees that frame the views of the ruins in the Museum Gardens are themselves interesting. The gardens were set up partly to increase knowledge so there are several very unusual trees here. An example is the big beech tree close to the Multangular Tower; it is sometimes called a "pear-barked beech" or "oak-barked beech" because it has rough bark above the obvious graft line on its trunk. It is registered as a "county champion" tree, which means it is the largest tree of its sort in Yorkshire – but as it may be unique this does not tell you much about its size! There are about seven "county champion" trees in the Museum Gardens.

St Mary's Abbey ruins beyond a 'pear-barked beech'

From the small gateway behind the Multangular Tower: as you stand in the gateway you will see a lawn to the left of the rough and rather damaged Roman wall, and at the far end of the lawn are the medieval ruins of the chapel and undercroft of St. Leonard's Hospital. At the near end of the lawn is the inside of the Multangular Tower with several Roman coffins in a coarse, hard sandstone called millstone grit. The medieval parts of the tower have arched embrasures to let longbow-men get up close to the arrows slits designed for them to shoot from. To your left the low Roman wall runs away from you towards a rough tower; here you are seeing what was under the medieval wall's ramparts until these were excavated. This Roman wall is about a metre into the city from the medieval wall that the gateway goes through. The walls of rounded cobbles are recent, built to line the excavations. For more about this area see "Off-trail extras: 4" on page 95.

From the square where the trail ends: on one side of the square you can see the railings of the King's Manor and a little of the manor itself, the late Victorian art gallery is on the next side, a wall and tower that defended St Mary's Abbey is on the next, and on the fourth side is a road backed by Bootham Bar. To the right of the bar on this road as you look at it are two very different frontages built at the time of the 1830s road, an officers' mess and then a theatre (the York Theatre Royal) – and between them a much admired modern extension to the theatre, housing its café.

Off-trail extras: 1. St. Leonard's passage

Immediately to your right after entering the Museum Gardens you can go 30 metres to a medieval, stone-vaulted passage that was once part of St Leonard's Hospital (for more about the hospital see "Off-trail extras: 4. Under the Walls" opposite. There are the foundations of a rounded Roman interval tower about 10 metres to your left just before you enter the passage. The passage is full of attractive information boards, the first on the left is the one most concerned with the Walls.

Off-trail extras: 2. Toilets and library

New public toilets are beside a new restaurant in the Museum – leave the trail by following the path that is the first on your left after entering the gardens, then go first left again and the toilets are about 30 metres ahead of you in a corner on your right. Alternatively there are toilets upstairs in the public library which is very close to the trail. To find the library, continue along the pavement instead of going into the Museum Gardens. After about 40 metres there is a small square containing the library on your left. As well as the toilets it has a café, York archives, displays about York, helpful staff, bookable computers for internet access, free wifi – and also books! Its quiet side lawn has a few benches and excellent ruins – see "Off-trail extras: 4" opposite.

Off-trail extras: 3. St. Mary's ruins

If you face the front of the Multangular Tower you may be able to see to your left the picturesque ruins of St Mary's Abbey church about 100 metres away.

The path that took you to the Multangular Tower will take you past the front of the Yorkshire Museum and onto these ruins. The museum was built in the 1820s, one of the first museums in the country; after a recent refit it must also be one of the most attractive. It allows close contact with many exhibits and is particularly good on Roman York and the parts of the medieval abbey that were discovered where the museum's lower floor is now. There is a charge for those who don't live in York.

St Mary's Abbey was founded in early Norman times and it held 50 monks following the Benedictine rule. It became one of the richest land owners in the north of England, partly because rich people gave it money and property in exchange for prayers that they believed would speed their souls through purgatory to heaven. As well as these prayers for the dead the Benedictine rule involved services every few hours through the day and night, conducted in the centre of their abbey's church. In the late 13th century they totally rebuilt the church. They built a big one; the windows you can see were down one side of the nave, which was about a quarter of the whole church. It was still in active use in 1539 when Henry VIII ordered its destruction. Nearly all "religious houses" (buildings housing monks, nuns or friars) were torn down at this time because they were a probable threat to the power of a king who had just got parliament to make him the head of the Christian church in England. Some monks were executed but St Mary's monks accepted pensions – and some of them also took paid work in Henry's new "Church of England".

In the centre of the ruined nave wall you may see many similar little hollows which are believed to be made by musket balls, possibly from the time there was close fighting here during the Civil War – attackers blew up a tower in the wall round St Mary's, stormed into these grounds and were then forced back. For more about the corner tower see "Off-trail extras: 6. St Mary's walls" on page 98.

To the right of the ruined nave wall, just the other side of where the centre of the church was, you can see the best of the garden's Roman coffins, some with words and images carved in their coarse sandstone.

Off-trail extras: 4. Under the Walls

At the little gate through the walls, the one described in "Basics" where you can look down at the inside of the Multangular Tower, you can go further. You will be wandering through the area described on page 93 as: *"From the small gateway behind the multangular tower:"* so it is best to read that description first before reading the extra details here. You may also wish to read the information board that is to your left, inside the gateway.

If you walk towards the ruins of St Leonard's Hospital you may notice, up against the very rough and damaged Roman wall on your right, the circular red brick base of a Roman oven (it is not on its original site). The stone vaulted undercroft of St Leonard's, and buildings that were where the lawn is now, were probably used for tending the sick – although the hospital was more involved in providing a home and food for the elderly and the poor. Augustinian canons, and women also following the Augustinian rule, worked and lived here throughout the Middle Ages until this religious house was destroyed in around 1540, as described previously.

If you walk back towards the Multangular Tower and turn right just before the steps then you will be walking along the inside of the Roman fort wall, the wall that turned a 90 degree angle at the tower. The Roman wall here was under the medieval ramparts until archaeologists excavated them; it is thought that similar walls are under the next 800 metres of ramparts – they are exposed again in part 1 of the east corner of the trail. At the end of this section of Roman wall you come to a small, roughly-built tower – this is a mystery called "the Anglian Tower". Anglians have left us very few buildings and it is now thought that this is late Roman work; in either case it is probably from a time when the fort walls were beginning to weaken and fall and someone built this rough extra tower with new stone from the hills north of York, rather than taking it from old walls or using the main Roman quarries near Tadcaster, west of York. It was the accidental discovery of this tower which led to the excavation of this bit of the ramparts. (These excavations sadly led to the death of an archaeologist when his trench collapsed on him). Beyond the little tower archaeologists have left us a labelled impression of how the ramparts under York's medieval walls were built up over the centuries. It may help you to understand the confusion of walls here if you realise that you have walked up the rough side of the Roman wall, the side the Romans piled an earth bank against. Its other side is the one faced with neatly squared stones which were known as "saxa quadrata". As you walked, on the other side of you were walls that probably belonged to St. Leonard's Hospital; the walls of rounded cobbles were built recently to keep you safe in the excavations by holding up the medieval city walls which stand tall here (but without any proper wall-walk along them). The rougher old walls here are usually full of wildflowers during the summer.

Off-trail extras: 5. Café at Kings Manor

The 80 metre walk to this café is so attractive you might wish to take it even if the café is not open. King's Manor university café is cheap, good and often quiet but usually it is not open at weekends or after about 3.00pm (3.30pm in term time). There is often a board with its opening times at the manor's gates in the square at the end of the trail.

To take this walk go through the gate; the lowest part of the building in front of you is the oldest in the very complicated set of buildings. The building to your right is the newest you'll see, it's from the early 20th century and successfully designed to fit with the rest. The doorway in front of you had its splendid royal coat of arms added by Charles I who was here just before civil war broke out in the 1640s. You'll notice that

Charles I coat of arms above the door to the King's Manor (off-trail extra)

Charles was very proud of the fact that his father and he were the first to be kings of England *and* Scotland, the Scots thistle and English rose are affectionately intertwined in this carving. His Lord President of the Council of the North lived here for a while and has his coat of arms carved in the equivalent place in the building that faces you when you go under the royal court of arms and through to the courtyard behind. (For more about this Lord President see "South Corner Part 1: Stories: Plague" on page 55).

When you are 10 metres in front of this second coat of arms the café is up the open air steps on your left, under another, more weathered carving of a royal coat of arms. This university courtyard and its quietness remind many people of the college courts and quadrangles of Oxford and Cambridge – in fact, though the age of the buildings is similar, York has only had a university since the 1960s.

Off-trail extras: 6. St Mary's walls

This "Off-trail extra" is mainly for those who are saddened to find themselves at the end of the trail round the Walls. Of course there's nothing to say you can't go round the Walls again but you might also like this last extra diversion.

St Mary's Abbey had its defensive walls built at the same time as the city's medieval walls but they have no earlier history so they are not built on top of ramparts. They are more masked by buildings attached to them than the city's defensive walls but such buildings have mainly been cleared away and a walk along the outside of these walls can be interesting and peaceful.

The first half of this walk is about 120 metres and worthwhile on its own. It goes along the near pavement of the busy street called Bootham and starts the other side of the late medieval tower at the edge of the square where the trail ends. This tower was built to guard a side gate to the abbey. A plaque tells you this gate was built for the convenience of Princess Margaret, the princess at the centre of the Bootham Bar story of the the two sheriffs, but it is now thought that it was really built for her father, Henry VII.

At first the walls past the tower are masked by buildings but when they appear briefly you can see simple masons' marks quite deeply cut into them. When they appear for the second time you can see more masons' marks, an interval tower and the rough stone the wall is built of behind the neatly cut facing blocks. When they appear for the third time it is at their round corner tower. You'll see facing you a dramatic scar down the side of this tower – this is a vivid reminder of the English Civil War.

You can see that to the left of this scar the walls are thicker with a slit window – they are medieval walls built for defence, but to the right of the scar the walls have been rebuilt thinner, for more peaceful times

St Mary's Tower at the corner of its walls (off-trail extra)

or times when thick walls and slit windows no longer brought security. The rebuild happened because in 1644 soldiers loyal to parliament dug a mine under this tower and exploded gunpowder in the mine, thus destroying the outer wall of the tower. When this wall fell, soldiers attacked here and round the corner, hoping to occupy the grounds of the King's Manor. Unfortunately for them they attacked without co-ordinating attacks from the other two parliamentary armies besieging York, so the defenders were able to concentrate all their forces on this one attack and it was driven back; many of the attackers were killed or captured.

The second part of this walk is almost double the distance and continues along the same pavement, turning left down quiet Marygate. Ten metres into Marygate look back at the tower to see the door-sized window that shows it once supplied guards to a wall-walk. Go about 40 metres on and you'll see an information board about the walls. It explains that battlements on the abbey walls had unusual swing-down, wood shutters to protect those shooting down from them. The merlons have grooves at the side, shaped like a dash with a small tail, so the shutters can be fitted and then swing. Two reproduction shutters can be seen in position here. The walk continues past more interval towers, past medieval St Olave's church, past the old main entrance to the abbey and down to the River Ouse and the round medieval tower beside it. This tower has good embrasures behind its arrow-slits to allow archers to get up close to them.

St Mary's defensive walls on the other two sides of its grounds have almost completely disappeared. You can walk back to the trail if you turn left when you reach the Ouse and then walk back to Lendal Bridge along its banks; or you can go through the small gate which soon appears on your left. This gate goes into the Museum Gardens close to the renovated, half-timbered, medieval, abbey "hospitium". If tradition is correct, it was a lodging house for travellers. The Multangular Tower and the trail are just to the right of the museum itself; the museum, built in the early 19th century to look a little like an ancient Greek temple, is about 120 metres behind the hospitium – it can be a pleasure to find your way there by paths or over the grass, though you may find the grassed flood defences between the gate and the hospitium too steep and slippery for you to go straight over the grass to the hospitium.

Stories: 1. Constantine the Great

Two sets of fathers and sons, all Roman emperors, lived in York for a while. Severus and his sons, from about 200AD, are scarcely remembered, though Severus was the first Roman Emperor from Africa and from his time we probably have the eastern corner tower of the Roman fort that we can still see. Emperor Constantius, in York about a hundred years later, is no better remembered but his son, Constantine the Great, is amongst the most famous and most important Roman emperors.

Constantius was the western emperor of a divided empire; he came to York to organise fighting against tribes in northern Scotland. The fighting was successful but he fell ill. His son joined him and when Constantius died his soldiers declared Constantine emperor in his father's place. It is believed that this declaration was in York in 306AD when the walls of the Multangular Tower were still new, presumably rebuilt in honour of the newly resident emperor, though some think they were from the time of Emperor Severus, a century before Constantius.

The soldiers had not cleared their declaration with the other emperors so Constantine had to fight for the title – but he did this so successfully that he re-united the Roman Empire under his leadership. It is said he fought with a Christian-like cross as his banner and the legend is that a vision showed him this cross in the sky with the words "in this sign, conquer". It certainly seems to be true that Constantine was very close to his mother, Helen, and that she had converted to Christianity, a religion that had faced a lot of persecution in the Roman Empire. Constantine stopped the persecution of Christians and, at the end of

Constantine's statue outside the Minster

his life he was baptised a Christian himself and left the empire poised
to adopt Christianity as its official religion. The Roman Catholic Church
has never looked back – or rather it was massively powerful from this
time onwards, and spent quite a lot of time and energy looking back
at the teachings of Jesus and infallible judgements of a line of popes
believed to stretch back to St Peter.

Stories: 2. A hole in the Walls

Close by the Multangular Tower the red stripe of the Roman wall has
been patched with newer non-Roman stone. Behind the patch there
is still a substantial hollow in the wall but there is disagreement on
the cause of the original hole. One bit of evidence is an old engraving
showing a substantial hole here and describing it as damage from the
Civil War – a Scottish army cannon demolished a corner tower half a
kilometre south of here and the same battery of guns could have made
this hole. Others say a house was attached to the inner side of the wall
here and the hole was knocked through for a window. I prefer to link
at least one of the hollows visible on the inner side of the wall to what
is usually called a Yorkshire folk tale. It is usually called a tradition but
it is sometimes told as the truth and it is sometimes explicitly linked
to St Mary's Abbey and St Leonard's Hospital, two institutions run by
different orders of monks yet separated by little more than this ancient
wall.

A brief version of the story tells that Brother Jocundus belonged to the
community of monks at St Leonard's. To be more precise, he belonged
to the community of Augustinian canons who ran St Leonard's Hospital
and he was a good enough canon except for a certain weakness for

strong drink. This weakness led to his being found drunk at a local fair and, as he was far from sober when asked to explain himself to the master of St. Leonard's, he caused so much offence that he was given a rather extreme punishment – he was taken to a convenient hollow in a wall at the edge of the hospital grounds and was walled-up in it, walled-up to die.

When he sobered up he was reluctant to die in this way so he loosened enough of the crumbling old stone work to get out of the wall and found himself on the other side of the wall from his fellow Augustinians. In fact he found himself in the Benedictine Abbey of St Mary's. Somehow, with little reference to the truth, he managed to persuade the Abbey to accept him as a novice monk. He was so relieved by his deliverance from death in the dark that he was able to stay away from strong drink for a whole year but then events repeated themselves. The abbot had him walled up in the same convenient hollow he had emerged from a year before. Jocundus, once sober, unsurprisingly attacked the wall the Augustinians had built up a year before; it was slow work but unexpectedly he soon had help from some of the same canons who had built the wall. His knockings and scrabblings had disturbed the monks in their quiet prayers for the soul of their master who had just died – they were astonished to find Jocundus alive and well after a year inside the wall. They declared it a miracle, a message from God that Jocundus should be their next master.

Monk-sized hole on the inside of the Roman wall (off-trail extra)

APPENDIX

TOURS

This guide is to help you enjoy a self-guided tour. Similar guidance (but a lot less detailed) is available via the VisitYork website and the York Archaeological Trust website. The trust sells an attractive colour printed version of their guide; as well as brief information on most of the City Walls Trail it explains some features that can no longer be seen. There is currently no other guidebook in print though the York Architectural and York Archaelogical Society (YAYAS) and Friends of York Walls may supply copies of the 1974 booklet "The Bars and Walls of York" through their websites.

Friends of York Walls' website tells you of tours you can arrange to have with their trained guides; it also plans to give you information that will keep this written guide up-to-date. Yorkwalk has a variety of regular walking tours with their professional guides, some including parts of the Walls. They set off from the main gates of the Museum Gardens and their website gives details.

The free tours led by members of the Association of Voluntary Guides for York usually include what is labelled in this guide as sections 1-3 and the later part of section 13. They set off from their A-board in the square opposite Bootham Bar at 10.15 everyday except Christmas Day (and often at extra times) and their website (www.avgyork.co.uk) gives more details.

Double-decker bus tours go round the outside of about half the Walls though currently not in winter. They often wait by Bootham Bar.

Various guides are available for mobile phones. What is available is changing fast so currently some advertisements are misleading; some of the material in some guides seems misleading too. *Walk along the City Walls* is a cheap app from Telltale Tours that you can download onto mobile phones. It has a rough map of most of the City Walls Trail and a lot of detail about ten of the towers and bars along the trail.

An audio-visual, interactive "virtual tour" of the Walls, partly coordinated with the guide you are now reading, is planned to be sold in 2014 by Actual Education and their website gives details.

STONE AND STONEWORK

The Walls are built almost entirely of magnesian limestone from near Tadcaster, about 10 miles south-west of York. This is a very variable stone but it often looks warmer, with more variable shades of light brown-yellow, than other uniformly white-grey limestones. This variable colour is partly because of the metal salts it contains. Its salts include the salts of magnesium that give the stone its name (other limestones are nearly all calcium carbonate) but it is probably when it contains iron salts that it has a warmer colour, and it seems to be the warmer coloured stone which turns red-pink when it is scorched by fire (a little like rust: iron oxide).

The stone was laid down at the bottom of a shallow, very salty bit of sea where few creatures lived so it has few fossils. While it was turning into rock it was unevenly soaked in chemicals; this soaking brought in the magnesium and iron, dissolved some shell fossils and made some bits of the rock very vulnerable to acid rain. Blocks made of this vulnerable rock have weathered fast since Victorian times, when smoke and engine fumes made the rain acid. Sometimes water soaks into it, rather than just washing over the surface, which causes the stone to flake off or turn to powder. Carvings and even the edges of arrow-slits on the Walls are more likely to get soaked and start "weathering" in this way.

When shell fossils have been dissolved even newly cut stone will have small holes in it. When there are small patches of vulnerable stone in a big block, these will become holes when the block weathers. These are two of the ways nature produces hollows in the stone of the Walls. These hollows can be mistaken for the scars of bullets and cannon balls but most people think there are real scars to be seen too.

The Romans used regular sized blocks a bit larger than a modern brick but the medieval masons used much larger, squared blocks of varied sizes. They both used lime mortar to cement the blocks together and used rubble and mortar as a thick filling sandwiched between two walls of shaped blocks. The medieval masons did not tie the two walls of shaped blocks together, so they tend to move apart – modern repairs use hidden metal ties.

The wall-walk paving is mainly what is now called "York stone". It is a brownish, fine-grained sandstone from the Bradford area about 30 miles south-west of York. It splits well into paving stones and probably got its name because it was so widely used in York's streets. On the wall-walk it was mainly laid in Victorian times. Unlike limestone it is particularly impervious to water so puddles form quickly on it and stay there. These puddles can become icy, which leads to the Walls being closed because the use of salted grit to melt the ice would increase the weathering of the limestone.

The Romans in York also used an orange-brown, coarse grained sandstone known as "millstone grit". They don't seem to have used it on the exposed bits of their fort walls but archaeologists say medieval builders of the Walls sometimes re-used Roman millstone grit. This is most obvious in the main old arch of Micklegate Bar. Millstone grit also seems to have been used by the Victorians to build some of their arches through the Walls. It comes from the edges of the Pennines; there are outcrops about 30 miles west of York.

Masons have sometimes left smaller scale signs of their work than the Walls themselves and the shapes and sizes of the blocks they cut and laid. Deep, drilled or chisel-cut holes 2-3 centimetres across were used for a lewis to grip in; a lewis is a metal device, used since Roman times to raise stones, which is attached to the end of a rope or chain instead of using a sling to hold the stone. These holes are rarely on a visible surface.

Mason's mark beside wall-walk (see page 69)

Where stones are not badly weathered, chisel marks, especially those showing the use of a "claw chisel" with a notched blade, are sometimes visible. More interesting and varied are "masons' marks". These are usually straight-line designs, some as simple as a triangle or arrow, cut using a knife or chiselled fairly lightly into stone blocks. They label a block as made by a particular mason and are in effect his signature in stone. It is thought stones were labelled for quality control, not so masons could be paid by output. At the time of the first building of the Walls there was a lot of building going on in York – the castle and the Walls were being built for fear of a war with Scotland, and the walls of St Mary's Abbey just outside the city were being built for fear of the Scots and fear of the people of York who were jealous of the monastery's wealth. The present Minster had been started a few years earlier and was still being built, so lots of wandering masons probably came to York. They would be strangers to the master mason in charge of the building so how was he to know their work was good enough to make them worth employing? So the practice was that each mason would have his own mark and he would sign his stones, or at least the stones he shaped first, with his mark so that the master mason could see the quality of his work. It is extraordinary that we can still see some of these marks after 750 years – because the mason who cut them only needed them to be visible for a few days. Several marks you can see are mentioned in the trail guide e.g. on pages 23 and 55.

FLOWERS OF THE WALLS AND RAMPARTS

The plants here are mostly the usual ones for an English roadside and rough wall.

A few plants grow in cracks in the Walls. One of the commonest and prettiest is the delicate ivy-leaved toadflax with small, lipped flowers of yellow and purple. It is also called "mother of thousands" because it can spread so well by seed. The seed heads move away from light so the seeds often go into cracks in the wall. It is from Italy and probably started escaping from English gardens in the 17th century. The yellow corydalis is a more showy, later escape from the garden. It has masses of strange, tube-shaped flowers and is native to the Southern Alps.

Plants like these do little harm, though any plant that roots in the Walls can start to push stones apart and plants that build up wood year to year, like Buddleia, have to be seen as beautiful enemies of the Walls.

In a few places ivy is growing on the walls and opinion is divided on the harm or good it does. Recent research suggests that it does good as long as its proper roots are not in the Walls (its aerial roots that just grip onto stone, seem to do no harm) – but it was cut back from the Walls east of Micklegate Bar in 2013.

Many daffodils have been planted on the ramparts so they make a fine show late-March to mid-April, lingering later in shady areas. Some people time their visits to York so that they come when the daffodils are in flower; it is said that the Romans brought daffodils to England, and some add that Roman soldiers carried daffodil bulbs to ease and speed their death if they were badly wounded, whilst others say it was to stick cuts together! The most obvious wild flowers on the ramparts are the tall, lacy white heads of cow parsley that flowers immediately after the daffodils. Their white and green is usually varied by a speckling of yellow, mainly from buttercups and dandelions. In the Minster grounds the Walls look down on typical English woodland flowers (like bluebells in May).

The greatest variety of wild flowers is usually found on the outer side of the rampart just east of Micklegate Bar. This is also where you can see, near the trees, the most historically intriguing plant of the ramparts: alexanders. This was probably introduced to Britain by the Romans and it was noted under the Walls in the 1780s. It was introduced as a spring vegetable and general tonic – all of it is edible: its umbels of tiny yellow flowers, its metre-tall celery-like stems, its glossy, dark green leaves and its black seeds. It is not common in Britain away from the coast, so it is tempting to think that it is here because Romans planted this "parsley of Alexandria" here.

Alexanders - brought by the Romans

On the outer ramparts west of the Micklegate Bar, and the inner ramparts east of the bar and near the railway station, hundreds of wild flowers were planted in 2012 to try to increase the variety of flowers. Look out for tansy, oxeye daisies, greater burnet, cowslip, knapweed, agrimony, clover and ladies bedstraw.

NAMES

The Bars

The main fortified gateways have been called bars (or barram or barre) since at least 1315 but in early times "lith" was used. To add a little confusion, a mid 12th century document refers to "Micklelith" (assumed to be Micklegate Bar) while having the word porta (Latin for gate) and barram in the same sentence. They barred the way – and may even have had a bar over which the murage tax was paid on goods being brought into the city for sale in its markets. Bootham Bar is a reference to the market booths outside it, where presumably traders didn't have to pay murage but had to pay something to the city as it became an official city market (although it was originally linked to St Mary's Abbey). The street there is also called Bootham. Walmgate Bar and Micklegate Bar are named after the city streets leading to them – "gate" is the name for street inherited from the Vikings and it is commonly used for old streets in north-east England. "Mickle" means big – a word probably shared by the Vikings and those they conquered here – so if you remember "many a mickle maks a muckle" as a proverb pointing out how little things accumulate, you should really correct this to "many a pickle maks a mickle".

Monk Bar is assumed to be named after some monks, perhaps some associated with the nearby Minster, but the Minster was never part of a monastery and though York had many "religious houses" run by monks none seem to have been close to this bar. There are two lesser bars: Victoria Bar was opened at the time Queen Victoria came to the throne (and probably is on the site of "Lounelith", the secluded bar); and one end of Fishergate, just outside Fishergate Bar (and Fishergate Postern), seems to have been the dam that made the river Foss into "the King's Fishpool". As mentioned in the trail guide, this dam was created on the orders of William the Conqueror; he was also known as "the Great King" and, less respectfully, as "William the Bastard".

The Towers

Starting at Bootham Bar and running clockwise around the trail, the towers you can see, as labelled by the Royal Commission on Historic Monuments, are in the north corner: 22, 23, 24, 25, 26, <u>Robin Hood Tower [27]</u>, 28;

in the east corner: Harlot Hill [31], <u>New Tower [32]</u>, 33, *34*, *Red Tower*, 35, 36;

in the south corner: 37, 38, <u>39</u>, *Fishergate Postern Tower*, *Clifford's Tower*, *Davy Tower*, *1*, 2, <u>Bitchdaughter Tower [3]</u>, 4, 5, 6, *Sadler Tower* [7], 8, 9, 10, 11;

and in the west corner: 12, <u>Tofts Tower [13]</u>, 14, 15, 16, 17, *Barker Tower*, *Lendal Tower*, <u>Multangular Tower</u>, *Anglian Tower* [19].

The last of these was not really part of the defences of the city in medieval times. The same could be said of the precinct walls of St Mary's Abbey but they are included as an off-trail extra in this guide. On an anti-clockwise walk round them starting at Bootham Bar, the towers are: Postern Tower, E, D, <u>St Mary's Tower</u>, C, B, A, *Water Tower*.

The underlined towers here are where the Walls change direction in a big way. The towers in italics are not interval towers – or do not look like interval towers at the moment – as they do not currently have the Walls on both sides of them.

We know earlier names for some of these towers but these seem of little interest except to specialist historians; the current names either have an obvious meaning and origin or are a puzzle. An exception is Clifford's Tower which probably started as an unofficial name (its earliest official use was in Elizabethan times), referring to the time when Sir Roger Clifford was hanging from it after being executed for taking part in an armed rebellion against Edward II in 1322. Some say his execution was by slow hanging from the tower. Other exceptions are Barker Tower (barkers used tree bark in the tanning of leather and they also used lots of water, so were probably based near this tower on the River Ouse; an area called Tanner's Moat is close by) and Lendal Tower. "Lendal" is a shortened distortion of "St Leonard's Landing" or "St Leonard's Landing Hill"; goods and people were landed from the Ouse beside the tower in front of St Leonard's Hospital.

INFORMATION BOARDS AND MARKERS

There are several different types of information board on the City Walls Trail but the commonest and most informative are the 18 orange and purple boards. 15 of the 18 main boards include a map showing most of the trail and an estimate of how long it takes to walk to the next boards in both directions along the trail. Some information on these is outdated – the phone number for example! Each bar has its large orange and purple board (Micklegate Bar has 2!) and most also have a section of a metal map you can take a rubbing off to build up a complete A4 map of the Walls and the old city inside them. The other boards and metal maps are mainly at the other places where you can get up onto the wall-walk.

There is only one information board on the wall-walk itself but there are a few places where you walk over words and symbols set into the stone. These tell you of something special to look at but they can be a bit of a puzzle. They have narrow frames which have a "V" cut out of them pointing in the direction you should look.

The route of the City Walls Trail between the lengths of walkable wall-walk is marked on the ground with small brass pavement studs showing a tower with battlements. Following these studs can be fun but it's more of a challenge than originally intended because a few

Two types of information board linked to the trail

Words and symbols set in stone - this one draws your attention to Baile Hill

have gone missing and 3 have even gone to the wrong side of a road (the city archaeologist planned to get these three removed in 2011 but city authorities act slowly in York – that's partly why we still have the Walls to walk round!) There seems to be no official map showing the whole studded route, with its two short diversions, but there's a leaflet version available to print on the Friends of York Walls website – and there is this guide you are reading! Glass marbles set in the pavement are part of a separate "Breadcrumbs" trail. Occasional small mosaics e.g. in the path west of the Multangular Tower (section 13) are mostly separate again.

On at least some parts of the wall-walk you may notice small brass markers embedded every 25 metres in the middle of the path. The easiest to spot, every 100 metres, are domed and a centimetre across; others are smaller and flatter, circular or hexagonal. These are simply to help those involved in maintenance to map problems that need attention.

REFRESHMENTS, SEATS AND TOILETS

These are usually mentioned in more detail as "Off-trail extras" in the trail guide; page references are given below in brackets.

There are many cafés, restaurants and pubs close to the Walls trail, what follows are brief details of some you might not notice or which are so special that you might want to plan to visit them.

Grays Court has its own steps down from the Walls into its splendid garden below the north corner of the trail, 100 metres north west of Monk Bar. It is fairly expensive, fair for its menu and surroundings – in the garden and in the house. For details (including use of its steps) phone 01904 612614 or go to its website. (Page 20).

In contrast, Keystones at Monk Bar is an ordinary pub but it has an excellent, sheltered, open air eating and drinking space set against the outer ramparts and is close by the old icehouse which is set into the ramparts. (Page 26).

In even greater contrast to Grays Court is the café of Morrison's supermarket. This is about 400 metres south-east of Monk Bar. It is close to the trail and easy to find as it's at the base of a chimney that is huge by York's standards and handsome by mine. Leave the trail by a part-pelican crossing (to your left when you are just past the closest point to the Victorian chimney), then go up a short path till you get to the chimney. (Page 37).

Another contrast is the small, wonderful, church-run café inside Walmgate Bar, usually open 10.00 – 6.00 though not on Sundays. Phone 01904 464050 or look at www.facebook.com/gatehousecoffee. Three of its small wonders, the barbican, portcullis and toilet, are behind the counter-bar – so ask if you wish to see them. (Page 47).

A fourth contrast is "The Postern Gate" (unsurprisingly next to Fishergate Postern Tower and beside the trail). This pub is run by Wetherspoons, so it has cheap food. It has a terrace looking out onto the River Foss and castle walls; it is in a modern building which I think fits in very well with its medieval neighbours. (Page 62).

The Bar Convent, café-restaurant, free museum and nunnery, is on the south-east corner of the crossroads just outside Micklegate Bar. It is in a fine Georgian building which also houses the oldest Roman Catholic nunnery in England. (Page 78).

On the west corner of the trail, Barker Tower, on the south bank of the River Ouse is about 20 metres of steps from the trail. This medieval tower has a small, excellent but toilet-less café called the Perky Peacock; currently it's not open at weekends or late in the afternoon. See www.facebook.com/theperkypeacock for further details. (Page 85).

King's Manor university café is cheap, often quiet and is in a fascinating old building but it is usually not open on weekends or after 3pm. It usually has a board out at the Manor's gilded gates in the square opposite Bootham Bar. (Page 96).

There are a few benches actually on the Walls – especially in the north corner, with half of them in the tower at that corner. The Walls trail goes past several benches in the beautiful but sometimes crowded Museum Gardens in the west corner of the trail, in the smaller and quieter Tower Gardens in the south corner, in the even smaller and quieter gardens by the Red Tower in the east corner, and in Exhibition Square opposite Bootham Bar. A lovely lawn-less garden with benches has recently been created just inside the Walls at Peaseholme Green in the east corner of the trail. The entrance to this is 80 metres from the Walls trail. You will find this easy-to-miss entrance on your right just before the Quilt Museum if you turn right along the pavement where the trail comes off the Walls, 300 metres south-east of Monk Bar. (Page 36).

The Victorians built toilets for men at every bar; these have gone but both sexes now have toilets at Bootham Bar. Just outside the Walls, 100 metres from Micklegate Bar, are the Nunnery Lane car park toilets (turn left, staying on the pavement as you leave the city by the bar). There are no public toilets near the other bars but when the trail turns away from Clifford's Tower, in the middle of the south corner, you can leave the trail by walking clockwise around the Tower, staying on the pavement and when the pavement ends with a car park entrance there are toilets 30 metres in front of you. There are new public toilets in the Museum Gardens – leave the trail by going first left after entering the gardens, then go first left again and they are about 30 metres ahead. The location of these and alternatives in the public library is explained on page 94.

Walmgate Bar's cafe: the door, the portcullis, the room upstairs

TIMELINE

The Roman Empire was growing. In 71AD the 9th legion came north and built a fort centred on where the Minster is now.

They built stone gateways (at least) for their fort. It was 400 by 500 metres, the base for 5,000 soldiers.

The Roman 6th legion built (or rebuilt) stone walls for the fort – probably when Emperor Severus and his family lived in York. A walled town had grown up opposite the fort, on the west side of the Ouse.

Some walls of the Roman fort were rebuilt, probably when Emperor Constantius was in York with his son, Constantine. A strong and showy wall faced the Ouse: two stripes of red tiles ran along the pale magnesian limestone wall and its tall protruding towers.

The Roman Empire got weaker, the legions were withdrawn to defend Rome. Britain entered the "Dark Ages", a time when we are not sure what happened to York's defensive walls.

Angles invaded and settled [coming from what is now Denmark], giving us the name, England.

In 627 King Edwin was baptised "under the lofty walls of the city of York... first built by Roman hands" according to Alcuin (writing in the next century).

In 867 Viking invaders captured Anglian York. At the time it was said that York's lack of strong walls led to this capture. The Vikings probably defended their "Jorvik" with earth banks and wood walls using half of the Roman fort's walls and extending them to the River Foss.

From 1066 William the Conqueror and his Norman army forced the English to accept him as King. He built castles to enforce his law. His two castles in York [built1068-9] became part of the circle of defences around the city - and so did the moats and lake he made by damming the Foss.

An extra earth rampart was built to protect the suburb of Walmgate on the east bank of the River Foss. Arched stone gateways were built through the ramparts.

In 1244 Henry III ordered York's wood castle to be rebuilt in stone. Fear of Scots and better siege machines led the city to build stone walls on its earth ramparts. City pride may also have been a motive.

A Scots army reached Bootham Bar in 1319, it didn't attack the Walls but it defeated an "army" of York people who chased after it. Monk Bar was built in its new position and the last of the Walls were built in stone.

A barbican and portcullis were added to each to each bar (as traders went through them they had to pay a tax to help maintain the walls). The Walls and bars were complete.

York people became short of money and work. Yorkshire anti-tax rebels damaged south-east Bars in 1489. Red Tower was built of brick by tilers to save money on stone. Masons harassed the tilers, probably murdering one. The present Fishergate Postern Tower was built to replace Fishergate Bar.

York's Walls were made ready to face the "Northern Rebellion" (of Roman Catholics against Elizabeth I, 1569-70)

The gaoler at Clifford's Tower stole its stones! York's corporation protested in 1596 &7 and he was stopped.

Charles I prepared York's defences to face Civil War armies supporting Parliament. He left an army here and York was besieged in 1644. Cannon and mining damaged the walls.

York's defences started to be pretty ruins in rich people's gardens or widened walks reminding the public of a dangerous past. Then "Bonnie Prince Charlie" invaded in 1745 - the Walls were hurriedly repaired! This scare over and some invaders executed, extra arches were created at the bars.

York's corporation [and then its council] wanted to open up York with new roads and then railways. It took down some bits of the Walls – many objected. A footpath society collected money and support to repair the Walls to be a public path. Slowly this society won over York's council. York's council restored the Walls for the public to use as a path.

In 1922 the Walls and other defences were made a "scheduled ancient monument" with legal protection.

Daffodils planted for celebrations and sad commemorations.

In 2011 Friends of York Walls formed with free membership to promote use and appreciation of the Walls.

GLOSSARY

Anglian: to do with people who took over the north of England (and gave England its name!) after the Romans withdrew. An Anglian king became Christian in York in 627AD.

bar: York's name for its main fortified medieval gateways (they *bar* the way into the city, they are a *bar*rier).

barbican: a big, defendable, front extension to a fortified gateway.

batter: a wall (or part of a wall) that slopes back rather than being vertical, sometimes at the base of thick, defensive walls.

coat of arms: a badge, usually symbols on a shield, identifying a particular individual, family, city etc.

common land: land that is reserved for everyone to use, where private building and fencing is not allowed.

corporation: the local people governing York from the early Middle Ages till around 1835 when a more democratic council took over.

council: unless more fully described, this is the organisation led by elected councillors with the power to govern local matters in York since 1835.

drawbridge pit: a pit to take the castle-end of a drawbridge when the bridge pivots into the up position (which leaves attackers without a bridge to cross).

embrasures: the low bits of a parapet with battlements; also where a wall is hollowed out behind a window e.g. to help an archer aim out of a slit window.

enfilading fire: shooting a set of attackers from the side so your shots run down the line of attackers.

garde-robe: a medieval term for what today is often called a toilet.

Georgian: to do with the times George I –IV were Kings (1714-1830).

Georgian-style: in this guide used for architecture using symmetrically placed largish windows which are mainly upright rectangles, with glass divided by wood glazing bars into smaller upright rectangles; also often using pillars linked by horizontals or round arches; with roofs that look flat or flattish.

Gothic: in this guide used for church architecture from the Middle Ages, buildings with tall, pointed arches to frame windows, doors and aisles.

keep: the building in a castle which is most heavily defended.

medieval: to do with the Middle Ages.

Middle Ages: in this guide used for 1150AD-1500 (but elsewhere often for 500AD to 1500).

merlons: the taller bits of a parapet with battlements.

musket loop: hole in a wall for a small gun to be fired through, muskets were like an early rifle but smooth bored.

Norman: to do with people from northern France who conquered England in 1066.

parapet: small wall protecting you from a fall – and from arrows etc.

pelican crossing: *pe*destrian *li*ght *con*trolled road crossing; the lights stop traffic when pedestrians press a button (the proper names for variants in these crossings are pelican, puffin, toucan and pegasus but in this guide they are all "pelican").

portcullis: a heavy gate that slides down in grooves to close. It usually has spikes at the bottom to fix it firmly in the earth.

postern: minor gate.

ramparts: defensive mounds of earth.

Roman: to do with the empire that was based in Rome and which controlled York from 71AD to about 400.

Victorian: to do with the time Victoria was queen (1837-1901).

Viking: to do with raiders, traders and settlers from Scandinavia who captured York in 866.

wall-walk: walkway high on a wall, running along the wall, usually behind a defensive parapet.

zebra crossing: striped road crossing where pedestrians have right of way at all times.

INDEX

References to maps are not included.

C

D

E

T

U

V

W

Y

York
   siege of **46–49**, 83, 89, 95, 98–99, 115
   Eye of 62-3
York Archaeological Trust 79, 103
York Art Gallery 10, 94
York charters 12, 76
York Gates 79
York Minster
   See Minster, the
York's coat of arms 9, 25, 77, 90
York stone 104
York Theatre Royal 94

Lightning Source UK Ltd.
Milton Keynes UK
UKOW06f1835211115

263246UK00001B/9/P